ON RAILWAY AND OTHER INJURIES OF THE NERVOUS SYSTEM;

ON RAILWAY AND OTHER INJURIES OF THE NERVOUS SYSTEM;

John Eric Erichsen

www.General-Books.net

Publication Data:

Title: On Railway and Other Injuries of the Nervous System
Author: John Eric Erichsen
General Books publication date: 2009
Original publication date: 1867
Original Publisher: Henry C. Lea
Subjects: Railroad accidents
Nervous system
Spine
Railroads
Nervous System
History / General
Medical / Neurology
Medical / Neuroscience
Medical / Orthopedics
Medical / Surgery / Neurosurgery
Transportation / Railroads / General
Transportation / Railroads / History

How We Made This Book
We automated the typing, proof reading and design of this book using Optical Character Recognition (OCR) software on a scanned copy of the original rare book. That allowed us to keep your cost as low as possible.

If the book is very old, worn and the type is faded, this can result in a lot of typos or missing text. This is also why our books don't have illustrations; the OCR software can't distinguish between an illustration and a smudge.

We understand how annoying typos, missing text or illustrations can be. That's why we provide a free digital copy of most books exactly as they were originally published. Simply go to our website (www.general-books.net) to check availability. And we provide a free trial membership in our book club so you can get free copies of other editions or related books.

OCR is not a perfect solution but we feel it's more important to make the book available for a low price than not at all. So we warn readers on our website and in the descriptions we provide to book sellers that our books don't have illustrations and may have typos or missing text. We also provide excerpts from each book to book sellers and on our website so you can preview the quality of the book before buying it.

If you would prefer that we manually type, proof read and design your book so that it's perfect, we are happy to do that. Simply contact us via our website for the cost.

CONTENTS

1

SECTION 1

INJURIES OF THE NERVOUS SYSTEM.

LECTURE THE FIRST.

Introductory Remarks – Injuries of Spine – Importance of Subject – Conflict of Professional Opinion not confined to Medical Profession – Necessity of Precision of Statement – The " Railway Spine" – Opinion of Surgeons – Bacon's Opinion – Case of Count de Lordat – Conclusion.

INTRODUCTORY REMARKS.

Gentlemen: It has justly been said by one of the greatest masters of the Art of Surgery that this or any other country has ever produced – Robert Liston – that no injury of the head is too trivial to be despised. The observation, true as it is with regard to the head, applies with even greater force to the spine; for if the brain is liable to secondary diseases in the one case, the spinal cord is at least equally, and probably more so, in the other.

My object in these Lectures will be to direct your attention to certain injuries and diseases of the spine arising from accidents, often of a trivial character – from shocks to the body generally, rather than from blows upon the back itself – and to endeavour to trace the train of progressive symptoms and ill effects that often follow such injuries.

These concussions of the spine and of the spinal cord not unfre- quently occur in the ordinary accidents of civil life, but from none more frequently or with greater severity than in those which are sustained by passengers who have been subjected to the violent shock of a railway collision; and it is to this particular class of injuries that I am especially desirous of directing your attention. For not only have they, in consequence of the extension of railway traffic, become of late years of very frequent occurrence, but, from the absence often of evidence of outward and direct physical injury, the obscurity of their early symptoms, their very insidious character, the slowly progressive development of the secondary organic lesions, and functional disarrangements entailed by them, and the very uncertain nature of the ultimate issue of the case, they constitute a class of injuries that often tax the diagnostic skill of the surgeon to the very utmost. In his endeavours not only to unravel the complicated series of phenomena that they present, but also in the necessity that not unfrequently ensues of separating that which is real from those symptoms which are the consequences of the exaggerated importance that the patient attaches to his injuries, much practical skill and judgment are required.

The secondary effects of slight primary injuries to the nervous system do not appear, as yet, to have received that amount of con centrated attention on the part of surgeons that their frequency and their importance demands; and this is the more extraordinary, not only on account of the intrinsic interest attending their phenomena, but also from their having become of late years a most important branch of medico-legal investigation. There is no class of cases in which medical men are now so frequently called into the witness- box to give evidence in courts of law, as in the determination of the many intricate questions that often arise in actions for damages against railway companies for injuries alleged to have been sustained by passengers in collisions on their lines; and there is no class of cases in which more discrepancy of surgical opinion is elicited than in those now under consideration.

It is with the view and in the hope of clearing up some of the more obscure points connected with these injuries, that I bring this important subject before you; for I believe that, as these cases come to be more carefully studied, and consequently to be better understood, by surgeons, much of the obscurity that has hitherto surrounded them will be removed, and we shall less frequently see those painful contests of professional opinion which we have of late been so often constrained to witness in courts of law.

That discrepancy of opinion as to relations between apparent cause and alleged effect; as to the significance and value of particular symptoms, and as to the probable result in any given case, must always exist, there can be no doubt, more especially where the assigned cause of the evil appears to be trivial, where the secondary phenomena develop themselves so slowly and so insidiously that it is often difficult to establish a connecting link between them and the accident.

And for the existence of such discrepancy of opinion, and for the expression of it, if necessary, on oath – as a matter of opinion, merely – a very undue amount of blame has been cast on members of the medical profession.

In well-marked and clearly-defined cases of injury, where the physical lesion is distinct – as in a fracture – 'or the general symptoms unmistakable, as in the loss of sight or hearing, or in the sudden and immediate induction of paralysis – no discrepancy of opinion can or ever does exist; and I have no hesitation in saying that in at least nineteen-twentieths of all the railway or other accidents that are referred to surgeons of experience for arbitration or opinion, there is no serious difference as to the real nature of the injury sustained, or as to its probable result on the patient, either locally or constitutionally, immediately or remotely. But in a certain small percentage of cases, in which, as has already been said, the relation between alleged cause and apparent effect may not always be easy to establish, in which the symptoms come on slowly and gradually, in which they may possibly be referable to other constitutional states, quite irrespective of and pre-existing to the alleged injury, and in which the ultimate result is necessarily most doubtful, being dependent on many modifying circumstances; in such cases, I say, discrepancy of professional opinion may legitimately, and indeed must necessarily, exist. There is no fixed standard by which these points can be measured. Each practitioner will be guided in his estimate of the importance of the present symptoms, and of the probable future of the patient, by his own individual experience or preconceived views on these and similar cases. But, in these respects such cases differ in no way from many others of common and daily occurrence in medical and surgical practice. We daily witness the same discrepancies of opinion in the estimate formed by professional men of obscure cases of any kind. In cases of alleged insanity, in the true nature and probable cause of many complicated nervous affections, in certain insidious and obscure forms of cardiac, pulmonary, and abdominal disease; in such cases as these we constantly find that *"quot homines lot sentential'* still holds good. Even in the more exact science of chemistry, how often do we not see men of the greatest experience differ as to the value of any given test, as to the importance of any given quantity of a mineral – as of arsenic, mercury, or antimony, found in an internal organ – as an evidence of poisoning.

Were public discrepancies of opinion confined to the members of the medical profession it would be a lamentable circumstance, and one which might justly be supposed to indicate a something deficient in the judgment, or wrong in the morale, of its members. But when we look around us, and inquire into the conduct of members of other professions, we shall find that in every case in which the question at issue cannot be referred to the rigid rules of exact science – whether it be one of engineering, of law, of politics, or of religion – the same conflict of opinion will and does, as a matter of necessity, exist, and the same subjects and the same phenomena will present themselves in very varying aspects to the minds of different individuals – conflict of opinion being the inevitable result.

Look at any great engineering question. Are engineers of the highest eminence not ever to be found ranged on opposite sides in the discussion of any point of practice that has become one of opinion, and that cannot be decided by a reference to those positive data on which their science is founded ? Is there no discrepancy of opinion often manifested amongst gentlemen of unimpeachable integrity in their profession, as to the possible causes of that very accident, perhaps, which has occasioned the catastrophe that has led to your presence in the witness-box ?

Is the law exempt from conflicts of opinion, independently of those that are of daily occurrence in its courts? Are there no such institutions as courts of appeal?

Are decisions never reversed? Are the fifteen judges always of one mind upon every point that is submitted to them ? Do we never see conflict of opinion spring up in the Lords and Commons, amongst the magnates of the legal profession, on questions that involve points of professional doctrine and practice?

Is the Church herself free from differences of the widest kind on questions that we are taught are of the most vital importance ? Have we not for years past heard questions of doctrine, of practice, of ritualism, discussed with an amount of vehemence and zeal to which we can find no parallel in our own profession ? Are not angry passions roused in quarters where they are little to be expected, and may we not at times be tempted to exclaim, " *Tanleene animis ccelestibiis irce* ?"

These conflicts of opinion, gentlemen, are common to all the professions and to every walk of life. Religion and politics, law, medicine, and the applied sciences, all contain so much that is, and ever must be, matter of opinion, that men can never be brought to one dead level of uniformity of thought upon any one of these subjects; and out of the very conflicts of opinion that are the necessary consequence of the diversity of views that are naturally entertained, Truth is at last elicited.

Far be it from me to do otherwise than to speak with the utmost respect of a learned and liberal profession, when I say that slight discrepancies of opinion arising between medical men are often magnified by the ingenuity of advocates, so as to be made to assume a very different aspect to that which they were intended to present, and are exaggerated into proportions which those who propounded them never meant them to acquire. Medical men deal habitually with the material rather than the ideal, with facts rather than with words, and are frequently, perhaps, at times somewhat inexact in the expressions they use. Mere verbal differences, mere diversities in modes of expressing the same fact, are thus sometimes twisted into the semblance of material discrepancies of statement and opinion. How often have I not heard in courts of law attempts made to show that two surgeons of equal eminence did not agree in their opinions upon the case at issue, because one described a limb as being "paralytic," whilst the other perhaps said "there was a loss of nervous and muscular power in it" – when one said that the patient " dragged" a lirnb, the other that he " walked with a certain awkwardness of gait." The obvious professional moral to be deduced from this is, that it is impossible for you to be too precise in the wording of your expressions when giving evidence on an obscure and intricate question. However clear the fact may be to your own minds, if it be stated obscurely, or in terms that admit of a double interpretation, you may be sure that the subtle and practised skill of those astute masters of verbal fence who may be opposed to you, will not fail to take advantage of the opening you have inadvertently given them, to aim a fatal thrust at the value of your evidence. It is your province to give a distinct and clear description of the facts that you have observed, and an unbiassed and truthful opinion as to the inferences you draw from them. It is their business to elicit the Truth, and to place the cause of their client in the best possible light, by questioning the accuracy of your facts and by sifting the validity of the opinions you have deduced from them.

I purpose illustrating these lectures by cases drawn from my own practice, and by a reference to a few of the more interesting published cases that bear upon the subject. In doing so, I shall confine myself to the detail of a few selected instances.

It would be as useless as it would be tedious to multiply them to any great extent, as they all present very analogous trains of symptoms and phenomena. I will not confine my illustrations to cases drawn from railway accidents only, but will show you that precisely the same effects may result from other and more ordinary injuries of civil life. It must, however, be obvious to you all, that in no ordinary accident can the shock be so great as in those that occur on railways. The rapidity of the movement, the momentum of the person injured, the suddenness of its arrest, the helplessness of the sufferers, and the natural perturbation of mind that must disturb the bravest, are all circumstances that of a necessity greatly increase the severity of the resulting injury to the nervous system, and that justly cause these cases to be considered as somewhat exceptional from ordinary accidents. This has actually led some surgeons to designate that peculiar affection of the spine that is met with in these cases as the *"railway spine."*

But yet, though the intense shock to the system that results from these accidents naturally and necessarily gives to them a terrible interest and importance, do not for a moment suppose that these injuries are peculiar to and are solely occasioned by accidents that may occur on railways.

There never was a greater error. It is one of those singular mistakes that has arisen from men trusting too much to their own individual experience, and paying too little heed to the observations of their predecessors. It is an error begot in egotism and nurtured by indolence and self-complacency. It is easy for a man to say that such and such a thing cannot exist, because, "I, in my large experience at our hospital, never saw it," and not to trouble himself to learn, by the study of their works, that surgeons of equally large, or perhaps of far greater, experience in their generation, have seen and have described it.

Sir Astley Cooper, who certainly enjoyed a wider range of experience in surgical practice than has ever before or since fallen to the lot of any one man in this country, said that his experience, extensive as it had been, was only as a bucket of water out of the great ocean of surgical knowledge.

In the writings of Sir A. Cooper himself, in those of his predecessors and contemporaries, especially of Boyer, of Sir C. Bell, and, at a later period, of Ollivier and Abercrombie, you will find many cases recorded that prove incontestably that precisely the same trains of phenomena that of late years have led to the absurd appellation of the "Railway Spine," had arisen from accidents, and had been described by surgeons of the first rank in this country and France, a quarter of a century or more before the first railway was opened, and that they were then generally recognized by surgeons as arising from the common accidents of civil life. The only difference being, that those accidents having increased in frequency and intensity since the introduction of railways, these injuries have become proportionally more frequent and more severe.

Bacon truly said, " They be the best physicians which, being learned, incline to the traditions of experience, or, being empirics, incline to the methods of learning." The same remark is applicable to surgeons, and that observation is as true at the present day as when it was made, nearly three hundred jears ago.

Yes, truly, gentlemen, if you are "empirics," incline to the methods of learning. Do not trust wholly to your empiricism;" in other words, to your own individual experience; but learn what has been seen by others of equal, perhaps of greater, experience than yourselves; as accurate in observing, and as truthful in recording. The study of the works of such men is not a vain and futile learning, but one replete with valuable results. In reading their works, you feel that you come into direct communion with these great men – with the Boyers, the Bells, and the Coopers – and from them you will learn many a lesson of practical wisdom, the direct result of their own accurate observations.

But you may go further back than the writings of these great men, and you will find scattered here and there throughout medical literature occasional most interesting cases that bear upon this very point. You will find much in this literature that anticipates what are often erroneously supposed to be more recent discoveries, and many a man, thinking that he has struck out a new vein of truth, and finding that it has already, years ago, been explored and the ore extracted by his predecessors, may exclaim, " *Perea. nl ante nos qui nostra dixere.*"

If you take up the third volume of the "Medical Observations and Inquiries," you will find that in 1766, exactly one hundredyears ago, a case is related by Dr. Maty of "a palsy occasioned by a fall, attended with uncommon symptoms," which is of so interesting a nature, and which bears so closely upon our subject, that I feel that I need no apology for giving you an abstract of it here, although, as it occurred between sixty and seventy years before the first railway was opened in this country, it might at first appear to have less relation to railway accidents than it really has, for it is identical in its course and symptoms with many of them.

This case, which is given at length, is briefly as follows: –

Count de Lordat, a French officer of great rank and merit, whilst on his way to join his regiment, in April, 1761, had the misfortune to be overturned in his carriage from a pretty high and steep bank. His head pitched against the top of the coach; his neck was twisted from left to right; his left shoulder, arm, and hand much bruised. As he felt at the time little inconvenience from his fall, he was able to walk to the next town, which was at a considerable distance. Thence he pursued his journey, and it was not till the sixth day that he was let blood on account of the injury to the shoulder and hand.

The Count went through the fatigues of the campaign, which was a very trying one. Towards the beginning of the winter (at least six months after the accident), he began to find an impediment to the utterance of certain words, and his left arm appeared to be weaker. He underwent some treatment, but without much advantage; made a second campaign, at the end of which he found the difficulty in speaking and in moving his left arm considerably increased. He was now obliged to leave the army and return to Paris, the palsy of the left arm increasing more and more. Many remedies were employed without effect. Involuntary convulsive movements took place all over the body. The left arm withered more and more, and the Count could hardly utter a few words.

This was in December, 1763, two years and a-half after the accident.

He consulted various physicians, and underwent much treatment without benefit.

In October, 1764, three years and a-half after the fall, Dr. Maty saw him. "A more melancholy object," he says, "I never beheld. The patient, naturally a handsome, middle-sized, sanguine man, of a cheerful disposition and an active mind, appeared much emaciated, stooping, and dejected. He walked with a cane, but with

much difficulty, and in a tottering manner." His left hand and arm were wasted and paralyzed; his right was somewhat benumbed, and he could scarcely lift it up to his head. His saliva dribbled away; he could only utter monosyllables, "and these came out, after much struggling, in a violent expiration, and with a low tone, and indistinct articulation." Digestion was weak, urine natural. His senses and the powers of his mind were unimpaired. He occupied himself much in reading and writing on abstruse subjects. No local tumour or disease was discoverable in the neck or anywhere else. From this time his health gradually declined, and he finally died on the 5th March, 1765, nearly four years after the accident.

On examination after death, the pia mater of the brain was found "full of blood and lymph;" and towards the falx some marks of suppuration. The medulla oblongata is stated to have been greatly enlarged, being about one-third larger than the natural size. The membranes of the cord were greatly thickened and very tough. The cervical portion of the cord was hardened, so as to resist the pressure of the fingers.

"From these appearances," says Dr. Maty, "we were at uo loss to fix the cause of the general palsy in the alterations of the medulla spinalis and oblongata." That the twisting of the neck in the fall had caused the membrane of the cord to be excessively stretched and irritated; that this cause extended by degrees to the spinal marrow, which, being thereby compressed, brought on the paralytic symptoms.

This case is of the utmost interest and importance; and though it occurred more than a century back, and was published exactly one hundred years ago, it presents in so marked a manner the ordinary features of a case of "concussion of the spine," arising from injury, that it may almost be considered a typical case of one of those accidents.

The points to which I would particularly beg to direct your attention in this case are these: –

1st. That there was no evidence of blow upon the spine – merely a twist of the neck in the fall.

2d. That no immediate inconvenience was felt, except from the bruise on the shoulder and hand.

3d. That the patient was able to walk a considerable distance, and to continue his journey after the occurrence of the accident.

2

SECTION 2

4th. The symptoms of paralysis did not manifest themselves for several months after the injury.

5th. They were at first confined to the left arm and to the parts of speech.

6th. They very slowly but progressively increased, extending to the left leg and slightly to the right arm.

7th. This extension of paralysis was very gradual, occupying two or three years. The sphincter were not affected, and the urine was healthy.

8th. The general health gradually but slowly gave way, and death at last ensued, after a lapse of four years, by a gradual decay of the powers of life.

9th. After death, evidences of disease were found in the membranes of the cord, and the cord itself. The narrator of the case stating that the membranes were primarily, and the cord secondarily, affected.

You will find, as we proceed in the investigation of this subject, that the symptoms, their gradual development, and the after-death, appearances presented by this case, are typical of the whole class of injuries of the spine grouped together under the one common term "Concussion," from whatever cause arising.

LECTURE THE SECOND.

EFFECTS OF SEVERE BLOWS ON THE SPINE.

Concussion of the Spine from Direct and Severe injury – Opinions of Authors, Cooper, Mayo, Bell, Boyer, Abercrombie, Ollivier – Case 1, Recovery – Case 2, Partial Recovery – Case 3, "Permanent Paralysis – Case 4, Death after Concussion of the Spine from Direct Injury to the Back – Effects of Severe Blows on the Spine – Fatal Result of Concussion of the Spine – Hemorrhage within Spinal Canal – Laceration of Membranes – Inflammation of Cord and Membranes – Cases – Complications of Injury of Cord – Rupture of Ligaments of Spine – Inflammatory Softening.

It is not my intention in these Lectures to occupy your time with any remarks on those injuries of the spine that are attended by obvious and immediate signs of lesion to the vertebral column itself, such as fractures and dislocations of it, or direct wounds of the cord. The nature and the consequences, proximate and remote, of such injuries as these are so obvious and so well understood by all engaged in surgical practice, that their consideration need not detain us.

My object is to bring under your observation the effects, local and constitutional, immediate and remote, of certain forms of injury to which the spinal cord may be exposed without lesion of its protecting column or enveloping membranes. These injuries, from the obscurity of their primary symptoms, the very slow development of their secondary phenomena, and from the ultimate severity and long persistence of the evils they occasion, are of the greatest interest to the practical surgeon.

In considering these injuries, I shall adopt the following arrangement : –

1. The consideration of the effects of slight and apparently trivial injuries applied directly to the spine.

2. The effects that injuries of distant parts of the body, or that shocks of the system, unattended by any direct blow upon the back, have upon the spinal cord.

3. The effects produced by wrenches or twists of the spine.

Before, however, proceeding to the consideration of these questions, it will, I think, be important to inquire into the effects produced by those forms of concussion of the spinal cord which follow immediately and directly upon a *severe* degree of external violence applied to the vertebral column, as by so doing we shall be able to understand more clearly the phenomena resulting from the slighter form of injury.

It is by no means easy to give a clear and comprehensive definition of the term, "Concussion of the Spine." Without attempting to do so, it may be stated, in explanation of this phrase, that it is generally adopted by surgeons to indicate a certain state of the spinal cord occasioned by external violence; a state that is independent of, and usually, but not necessarily, uncomplicated with any obvious lesion of the vertebral column, such as its fracture or dislocation – a condition that is supposed to depend upon a shake or jar received by the cord, in consequence of which its intimate organic structure may be more or less deranged, and by which its functions are certainly greatly disturbed, various symptoms indicative of loss or modification of innervation being immediately or remotely induced.

Tn fact, it appears to me that surgeons and writers on diseases of the nervous system have included four distinct pathological conditions under this one term, "Concussion of the Spine," viz., 1. Ajar or shake of the cord, disordering, to a greater or less degree, its functions, without any obvious lesion cognizable to the unaided eye. 2. Compression of the cord from extravasated blood. 3. Compression of the cord from inflammatory exudations within the spinal canal, whether of serum, lymph, or pus; and, 4. Chronic alterations of the structure of the cord itself as the result of impairment of nutrition consequent on the occurrence of one or other of the preceding pathological states, but chiefly of the third. These various conditions differ remarkably from one another in symptoms and effects, and have only this in common that they are not dependent upon an obvious external injury of the spine itself, as the laceration or compression of the cord by the fracture or dislocation of a vertebra.

Concussion or commotion of the spinal cord as a consequence of severe and direct blows upon the back is an injury that has long been recognized and described by those writers who have occupied themselves with the consequences of accidents applied to this part of the body.

Sir A. Cooper1 relates two cases of concussion of the spine, one terminating at the end of ten weeks in complete, the other in incomplete recovery.

Mayo relates two cases. In one at the end of six months there was no amelioration. In the other at the end of four mouths symptoms of inflammatory softening of the cord set in.

Sir Charles Bell3 relates two most interesting cases of concussion of the spine, both occasioned by falls and blows upon the back, in one of which the symptoms were immediate, in the other only developing themselves slowly after an interval of some months.

Boyer4 relates two cases. In one the patient struck his loins by falling into a deep ditch. He was affected by complex paraplegia, and speedily died. On examination no morbid appearances could be detected, neither fracture, dislocation, effusion, or any lesion of the cord or its membranes. In the other case, a man amusinghimself with gymnastic exercises strained his back between the shoulders. He became paraplegic, and died in a few weeks. After death no lesion of any kind was found in the spine or cord.

1 Dislocations and Fractures of Joints, 8vo. ed., p. 526 *at seq.* i Outlines of Pathology, I, ond. 1836, 1 Surgical Observations, London, 1816. ' Maladies Cbirorgicales, vol. Hi. p. 135.

Abercrombie, in his well-known and philosophical treatise on the Brain and Spinal Cord1 has a short chapter on this injury, in, which he relates several cases from his own observations and from the practice of others, in which the characteristic symptoms of concussion of the cord followed blows upon the spine.

Ollivier2 has collected, from his own practice and that of others, thirteen cases of this injury. They are detailed with much minuteness. Several of these proved fatal, and of these the after- death appearances are given at length.

Concussion of the spine from a direct and severe injury of the back may terminate in four ways: 1. In complete recovery after a longer or shorter time. 2. In incomplete recovery. 3. In permanent disease of the cord and its membranes; and, 4. In death.

The probability of the termination in recovery does not depend so much on the actual severity of the immediate symptoms that may have been occasioned by the accident as on their persistence. If they continue beyond a certain time, changes will take place in the cord and its membranes which are incompatible with the proper exercise of its functions.

The following cases will illustrate these forms of spinal concussion from the infliction of severe and direct injury to the spine. The first case is an instance of complete recovery – after severe and uncomplicated concussion of the spine. The second case is one of partial recovery after incomplete paralysis from concussion. The third case is a remarkable instance of incurable paraplegia following concussion; and the fourth case is one of death following a direct blow on the spine.

Case 1. – A man, 42 years of age, a clerk, fell whilst getting down from the roof of an omnibus, striking his back heavily upon the ground. He tried to get up, but was unable to do so, and was carried to University College Hospital where he was admitted in February, 1857, under my care.

On examination it was found that he had a transverse bruise upon the back, in the dorso-lumbar region, probably from comingin contact with the step of the vehicle in his fall. He suffered pain on pressure about the bruised part; but there was no irregularity to be detected in the line of the spinous processes or any other sign of fracture or of injury to the vertebrae. The ecchy- mosis extended over the two or three last dorsal and the first lumbar vertebra. His consciousness was in no way disturbed. He could not stand, his legs giving way under him. He complained of complete numbness in the left leg, but in the right there was a certain degree of sensibility associated with tingling, pricking sensations. When laid in bed he could not move the left lower extremity, but he could flex the right thigh upon the abdomen and draw up the knee, though he could not raise the foot. The catheter was passed and clear urine drawn off.

i London, 1828, p. 375.

' Tniitc ds Maladies de la Moelle Epinlere. Paris, 1837.

He was ordered complete rest in bed; five grains of calomel, to be followed by a purgative enema, and the use of the catheter, if necessary, every eighth hour.

Febrile reaction set in, which continued for three or four days. He was quite unable to empty the bladder; the urine was consequently drawn off by the catheter. There was no incontinence of flatus or of feces. No change in the state of the lower extremities.

At the end of a week he was decidedly better; he could raise the right foot from the bed, and the normal sensibility of that limb had in a great measure returned. He could draw up the left knee, and there was some sensation in the leg and in the dorsum of the foot. The retention of urine continued.

At the end of a fortnight motion and sensation had returned in the right lower extremity, but the left limb was still weak and partially numb, with formications and tinglings. He now began to pass his urine – which was acid – without the use of the catheter. During the whole of this period the only treatment that had been adopted was rest in bed, with an occasional aperient. He was now ordered to sit up, and had dry cupping to the lower part of the spine.

At the expiration of another week he was able to move about on his feet with a tottering, straddling gait, by the aid of a chair and stick. He now steadily improved both in appearance and in power of moving. At the end of the first month he could walk with but little assistance; he was still very weak in the left leg, which was partially numb; it felt as if asleep, and tingled.

Stimulating embrocations were ordered to the spine, and he was put on the bichloride of mercury, gr. *2,* in tinctures cinchonas co. 3i, thrice a day. Under this treatment he steadily improved, and was able to leave the hospital at the end of the sixth week, walking with the aid of a stick. He was treated as an out-patient with strychnine and iron, and the local application of galvanism, for two or three weeks longer, and then dismissed cured.

This case is related as an instance of not very uncommon occurrence, in which, after a severe and direct blow upon the spine, paraplegic symptoms are suddenly developed, which again disappear completely in the course of a few weeks under the influence of rest and appropriate treatment. , The only point of special interest in this case is, that although there was paralysis and complete retention, the urine continued acid throughout. It is probable that the pathological lesion in such a case as this, consists of some intra- vertebral extravasation of blood, the compression exercised by which occasions the symptoms, which disappear as it gradually becomes absorbed.

Case 2. – A painter, 30 years of age, was admitted into University College Hospital under my care, in June, 1865, under the following circumstances. He states that whilst painting a house he overreached himself, and fell with the ladder to the ground, a height of about thirty feet, striking his back upon a gravel walk. His hand was cut in the fall but his head was uninjured. On admission he was found somewhat collapsed, cold, and with a feeble pulse. There was no evidence of fracture either of spine or pelvis, but the back was ecchymosed to some extent about the centre of the dorsal region. He could not stand, but when lying in bed could draw up the knees nearly to a right angle, although he was unable to raise the feet. He complained of numbness and tingling in both legs and feet, but could feel when pinched or pricked. The patient had perfect control over his sphincters, and the urine was acid.

He was treated by rest in bed, dry cupping to the spine, and occasional aperients. At the end of a month he had not improved, being as nearly as possible in the same state as on admission. He was now pat on small doses of the bichloride of mercury in bark, and had counter-irritation applied to the spine. Some little amendment took place under this plan of treatment, and in August he was able to sit up, but could neither walk nor stand without support, and continued to complain of the numbness and tingling in his legs. Towards the end of the month he seemed to have acquired slight power over the legs, and could manage, by dragging them along, and leaning on a chair and stick or crutch, to move across the ward. He now very slowly improved, and by the end of September was able to leave the hospital. He was emaciated, cachectic- looking, and could barely manage to walk and drag his leg, by holding on to the furniture, or by pushing a chair before him. He continued through the winter mending but slowly. Towards the early part of the following year he was taken charge of by the Sisters of Mercy, who sent him to their establishment at Clewer. There he gradually regained a certain degree of health and strength. I saw him again on April 20th, exactly ten months after the accident; he was then in the following state: –

He describes himself as being languid, depressed, and as if going out of his mind. His memory has become very bad – at times all seems a blank to him. When he goes on an errand he often cannot recollect what it is about; is always obliged to write it down. His thoughts are confused; he often mixes up one thing with another. He is very nervous and easily frightened. He dreams much, and is. told that he talks and cries out in his sleep.

He is "not the same man that he was," and thinks he never will be. He cannot do ordinary work as before the accident – only "odd jobs." He cannot walk more than a mile; cannot carry a pail of water without great exertion.

He is never free from an aching, throbbing pain in the back; most severe in the middle dorsal region. There the spine is very tender on pressure, and the tenderness extends to some distance on either side of it, more especially on the left. This pain is greatly increased by movement of any kind, especially by bending backwards. He stoops with great difficulty, and is obliged to go upon one knee in order to pick anything off the floor. He walks in a shuffling, unsteady manner, and always uses a stick. He complains of numbness and "pins and needles" in the right leg and foot. There is no difference in the size of the limbs.

He has suffered since the accident from muscas volitantes and coloured spectra, " like the rainbow" before his eyes. Light does not distress him, but loud noises do. His hearing is very acute indeed.

No irritability of bladder; holds and passes his water well; urine is acid.

This case presents a good example of concussion of the spine followed by partial paralysis of sensation and motion of the lowerlimbs without affection of the sphincters or alkalinity of urine, terminating in incomplete recovery.

It appears to me doubtful whether intra-vertebral hemorrhage took place in this case; but there can be little doubt that the spinal cord had sustained some serious organic lesion which interfered with complete recovery.

In some cases, however, the result is not so satisfactory even as in this; the symptoms that are immediately developed continuing for many years, even for the remainder of the patient's life, without change.

The following1 is one of the most remarkable cases on record, of long persistent paralysis after a blow on the spine, the loss of sensation being so complete that the patient submitted to the amputation of both thighs without feeling the slightest pain. As this case has never, I believe, been published in this country, and is of so very remarkable a character, I have thought that it might not be out of place to give an abstract of it here.

Case 3. – A man, 22 years of age, in felling a tree, was struck on the back part of the head and between the shoulders by a large bough. This accident occurred in 1845. The force of the blow expended itself chiefly on the lower cervical spine and the shoulders. A complete paralysis of sensation and motion, of all the parts below this, was the immediate result. This condition continued without the slightest change. The vital and animal functions were naturally performed. Respiration, circulation, digestion, secretion, and assimilation were all normal. There was a sensible increase in the frequency and volume of the circulation, and respiration was noticed to be slightly increased in frequency above the normal standard. The weight of the body became greater after than it had been before the injury, and the lower limbs retained their natural heat and physical development.

The patient evidenced an unusual share of mental vigour after the injury, and possessed a resolution and determination that are described as truly surprising in his helpless condition. He threw himself into the midst of society for excitement, and was fond of travelling, lying on his back in his carriage.

In 1851, six years after the accident, he presented himself in theCounty Medical Society (Greene, New York), and requested the amputation of his lower extremities, which he stated were a burdensome appendage to the rest of his body, causing him much labour in moving them, and stating that he wanted the room they occupied in his carriage for books and other articles. He insisted on the operation with his wonted resolution and energy. The surgeon whom he consulted at first refused to consent to amputation, not only objecting to so extensive a mutilation for such reasons as he gave, but fearing lest the vitality of the vegetative existence enjoyed by his limbs might be insufficient for a healthy healing process- The patient, still determined in his resolve to have the limbs cut off as a useless burden to the rest of the body, sought other advice, and at last had his wishes gratified.

1 Eve's Surgical Cases, p. 90; and New York Journal of Medicine, 1853. By Wiii. D. Purple, M. D., of Greene, New York.

Both limba were amputated near the hip-joints, without the slightest pain or even the tremor of a muscle. The stumps healed readily, and no unfavourable symptoms occurred in the progress of perfect union by the first intention. In this mutilated state he was perfectly unable to move his pelvis in the slightest degree. He resumed his wandering life, and travelled over a great part of the States. He died in May, 1852, of disease of the liver, brought on by his excesses in drink, to which he had become greatly addicted since his accident. No post-mortem examination was made.

This case is a most remarkable one in several points of view, and in none more than in this, that a double amputation of so serious a character could be successfully practised on a person affected by complete paraplegia, and yet that the stumps healed by the first intention. Besides this remarkable fact, there are two special points of interest in this case which bear upon the subject that we are now considering, viz., that the weight of the body is stated to have increased after the accident, and that the limbs which were so completely paralyzed as to admit of amputation without the patient experiencing the slightest sensation of pain, had in no way wasted during the six years that they had been paralyzed, but retained "their normal physical development," as is expressly stated in the report of the case. We can have no stronger evidence than this to prove that mere disuse of a limb for a lengthened period of years even, is not necessarily followed by the wasting of it.

Case 4. – J. E., a clerk by occupation, was admitted under my care into University College Hospital, October 2d, 1862. He had been knocked down half an hour previously by a Hansom cab, thehorse falling partly upon him, and striking him with its knee on the neck. He never lost consciousness, but being quite unable to move, was carried to the hospital; on his way he passed his urine and feces involuntarily.

On examination after admission, it was found that he had an abrasion and ecchymosis on the left side of the neck. There was no inequality or irregularity about the spinous processes, or any evidence of fracture of the spine, but the patient complained of severe pain at the seat of the bruise. There was complete paralysis of sensation and of motion in the lower extremities and the trunk as high as the shoulders – incontinence of feces, retention of urine. The breathing was wholly diaphragmatic. He was quite conscious, and gave a description of the accident. He had suffered from ure- thral stricture for thirty-three years, so that only a No. 5 catheter could be passed.

On the following day his state was much the same. He complained of great pain in the right arm and hand, which were bruised. He said he thought he was paralyzed, as he could not move his legs; but on being pressed to do so, after some difficulty be succeeded in raising both legs, and in crossing them. Sensation appeared to. be completely lost. His most distressing sensation was a feeling of tightness as of a cord tied tightly round the abdomen below the umbilicus.

5th. He had slept well, and was able to move his legs with less difficulty. Pulse 64, strong; passes feces involuntarily. Urine drawn off, and is ammoniacal. He was placed on a water mattress, as his back was becoming excoriated. Ordered quinine and acids.

8th. Is able to move his head and neck from side to side. Has less pain. Urine more ammoniacal; feces pass involuntarily. Bedsores over sacrum have much extended.

10th. Difficulty of breathing came on, but was relieved by the llth. On the 12th it returned, with mucous rales, and he died that night – ten days after the accident.

On examination after death the head and brain were found uninjured and healthy. On exposing the vertebral column, it was found that the sixth and seventh cervical vertebrae had been separated posteriorly. The vertebras themselves, and their arches, were quite sound, but there was a fissure without any displacement, extending through the articulating processes on the left side. A large quantity of blood was extravasated into the spinal canal, lyingbetween the bones and the dura mafer. There was a considerable quantity of reddish serous fluid in the arachnoid. The pia mater of the cord had some blood-patches upon it on the lower cervical region. The cord itself was quite healthy.

In this case it will be observed that the paralysis was most extensive, as much so as is compatible with life. The loss of sensation appeared to be more complete than that of motion, the patient being able, by an effort of the will, to cross his legs, but he could not feel when they were pinched or pricked. The fracture of an articulation without displacement was an accidental and insignificant complication, the real injury consisting in the extravasation . of blood within the vertebral canal, which, by compressing the cord, induced the paralysis, that ultimately proved fatal. Death being, doubtless, hastened by the effusion of a large quantity of serous fluid from the irritated arachnoid.

The primary symptoms of concussion of the cord immediately and directly pro- duced by a severe blow upon the spine will necessarily vary in severity and extent according to the situation of the injury, the force with which it has been inflicted, and on the amount of organic lesion that the delicate structure of the cord has sustained by the shock or jar to which it has been subjected.

A severe blow upon the upper cervical region may produce instantaneous death.

A severe blow inflicted on the dorsal region may induce more or less complete paraplegia.

In some cases the paralysis of the lower limbs has been complete and instantaneous; has affected both sensation and motion, with loss of power over the sphincters.

In other cases there has only been paralysis of motion, sensation continuing perfect.

The reverse has been met with, but less frequently and less completely, there being loss of sensation and impairment, though not complete loss of power over motion.

One leg is frequently more severely affected than the other. Or the two legs may be unequally affected as to sensation and motion; both sensation and motion being impaired, but in varying degrees in the two limbs.

There may be complete loss of power over the sphincters both of the bladder and anus, with incontinence or retention of urine and feces; or the loss of power may be confined to the bladder only. This is especially the case when there is paralysis of motion rather than of sensation in the lower limbs.

The state of the urine will vary. If there is no retention, it will continue acid. When there is retention the urine usually becomes alkaline, but sometimes even when there is complete retention it remains strongly acid; and Ollivier has noted the very remarkable circumstance in one case of retention that there was an enormous formation of uric acid, so that the catheter became loaded with it.

Priapism does not occur in concussion, as it does so often in cases of laceration and irritation of the cord.

The temperature of the paralyzed parts is generally notably lower than that of the healthy parts of the body, and in some cases an absence of normal perspiration has been observed.

The *secondary* symptoms of severe concussion of the spine are usually those of the development of inflammation in the meninges and in the cord itself. They consist in pain in some part or parts of the spine, greatly increased by pressure and on motion, consequent rigidity of the vertebral column, the patient moving it as a whole. The pain is greatly increased by all movements, but especially by those of rotation.

It frequently extends down the limbs or around the body, giving the sensation of a cord tied tightly.

If the case goes on to the development of acute inflammatory action in the cord and its membranes, spasms of a serious character come on – at first, usually of the nature of trismus – then general spasms of the body and limbs, usually followed by speedy death from the exhaustion produced by the repetition of these violent convulsive movements.

If the inflammatory action assume a chronic and subacute character, permanent alterations in the structure of the cord will ensue, which will lead to paralytic affections of an incurable nature, usually confined to the lower extremities, but sometimes influencing the brain, and associated with great and deep-seated derangement of the general health.

Concussion of the spine from a severe and direct blow upon the back may prove fatal at very different periods after the injury. The time at which death occurs will depend partly on the situation of the blow, and in a great measure on the lesions to which it has given rise.

Concussion of the spine may, and often has, proved fatal by thesudden induction of paralysis, without there having been found after death any lesion of the cord that could explain the fatal termination of the case.

Abercrombie says: " Concussion of the cord may be speedily fatal without producing any morbid appearance that can be detected on dissection." And he refers to the case related by Boyer, and four by Frank in confirmation of this remark.

But in other cases the fatal result may have been occasioned by direct and demonstrable lesion of the spine or cord.

There appear to be four forms of lesion that will lead to a fatal result in cases of spinal concussion.

1. Hemorrhage within the spinal canal.

2. Laceration of the membranes of the cord, and extravasation of the medullary substance.

3. Disintegration and perhaps inflammatory softening of the cord. 1. Hemorrhage within the spinal canal may occur –

1st. Between the vertebrae and dura mater;

2d. Between the membranes and the cord;

3d. In both situations.

In these respects intravertebral extravasations resemble closely those that occur as the result of injury within the cranium. The three following cases are illustrations of these three forms of hemo- rachis.

Sir A. Cooper mentions one case, to which I shall have occasion hereafter to refer, in which, in consequence of a strain of the neck in a boy of 12 years of age, symptoms of paralysis slowly supervened, which proved fatal at the end of a twelvemonth.

On examination after death, " the theca vertebralis was found overflowing with blood, which was effused between it and the inclosing canals of bone." This extravasation extended from the first cervical to the first dorsal vertebra.

Miiller1 relates the case of a corporal of cuirassiers who fell from a hay-loft on to his back, striking it against a log of wood. He was found to be completely paralyzed in his lower limbs, but preserved his consciousness. He died on the second day. On examination it was found that there was a large quantity of blood extravasated between the spinal cord and its membranes. This extravasation extended from the sixth cervical to the ninth dorsal vertebra.

1 Bull, des So. M6dicales, 1826.

Ollivier1 relates the case of a woman 49 years old, who threw herself out of a window in the fourth story, alighting on her back. There was complete paralysis of the lower lirnbs, with incontinence of urine. Her mental faculties were unimpaired. She died on the third day after the injury, and on examination it was found that there was a fracture, but without any displacement, of the tenth dorsal vertebra; at this spot blood was extravasated between the vertebra and the dura mater, and also into the subarachnoid cellular tissue.

2. Death may occur – in that form of severe concussion which we are at present considering – from laceration of the pia mater, and hernia of the cord. Of this form of fatal result, Ollivier records one case, that of a man, 46 years of age, who had fallen heavily on his back, striking the spine in the middle of the dorsal region. He had paraplegia, paralysis of the sphincters, violent pain in the spine at the seat of injury, and much constitutional disturbance. He died on the seventeenth day. On examination after death it was found that the pia mater of the cord had been ruptured at two places opposite to the seat of injury, giving exit to the medullary substance in two patches, each about the size of a halfpenny, about two to three lines in thickness, and of a reddish colour. These protrusions had passed out of two longitudinal slits

in the meninges of the cord, each about one inch in length, situated at the medial and posterior part, and opposite to the fourth and fifth dorsal vertebrae. At the points opposite to these herniary protrusions, the spinal cord was much contracted, having lost a great part of its substance; but it preserved its normal consistence. The dura mater contained a large quantity of bloody serum.

3. The last condition of the cord that leads to a fatal termination in these cases of concussion arising from direct and severe injury is an inflammation, with, perhaps, suppuration of the meninges, with inflammatory softening and disintegration of its substance. This is, doubtless, of an acute and probably inflammatory character. The following cases will illustrate the morbid state.

Ollivier relates the case of a man, 28 years of age, who fell from the second story of a house, striking himself violently on his back, left hip, and thigh. His lower extremities became paralyzed completely, so far as motion was concerned ; incompletely, as to sensation. The sphincters were paralyzed. He died on the thirtieth day after the accident. On examination after death, it was found that the spinous process of the fourth cervical vertebra was detached but not displaced, and the twelfth dorsal vertebra was broken across but not displaced. The spinal cord was healthy in all parts except opposite this point, where it was soft, diffluent, of a yellowish-gray colour, and injected with capillary vessels.

' Vol. i. p. 492.

A remarkable case is recorded by Sir C. Bell (op. cit., p. 145). It is that of a wagoner who was pitched off the shafts of his cart on to the ground, falling on his neck and shoulders. At this part there was evidence of bruising. He could not stand, and dragged his legs. He lay for nearly a week without complaint, and had during this time no sign of paralysis. But on the eighth day he was suddenly seized with convulsions over the whole of the body – which were relieved by bleeding. He became maniacal, but in the course of twelve hours the convulsions ceased and he became tractable. On the third day after this attack he complained of difficulty in using his arm, and on the fifth day he had total palsy of the lower extremities, regaining the use of his arm. He died about a week after this. On examination after death, it was found that a considerable space existed between the last cervical and the first dorsal vertebra. The intervertebral substance was completely destroyed, and an immense quantity of pus surrounded the bones. This purulent collection had dropped down through the whole length of the sheath of the cord to the *cauda equina.*

The following case offers a remarkable resemblance to the preceding one – being attended by nearly identical post-mortem appearances following the same kind of injury.

13r. Mayes,1 of Sumter District, South Carolina, relates the case of a negro who, while raccoon-hunting, fell a height of fifteen feet from a tree, striking his back at the lower cervical and upper dorsal region against the ground. He instantly became completely paraplegic, and died on the tenth day. On examination seven hours after death, it was found that the fifth and sixth cervical vertebrae were separated from each other posteriorly, but not fractured or dislocated. Here there was manifest injury to the medulla. As soon as the muscular coverings of the spine were cut through, the softened and disintegrated medulla gushed out "similar to theescape of matter from an abscess when opened by the lancet. The medulla spinalis was evidently at this point in a state of decomposition."

1 Southern Medical and Surgical Journal, 1847.

In this case it is evident that not only the meninges of the cord, but the ligamenta subflava were torn through, and the arches of the vertebrae separated to such an extent, that the softened and disorganized medulla found a ready exit through the gap thus made at the posterior part of the spinal column.

It is a point of much practical moment to observe that in this, as in several other of the cases of so-called "concussion of the spine," there is, in addition to the lesion of the cord, some serious injury inflicted on the ligamentous and bony structures that enter into the composition of the vertebral column, which, however, must be considered as accidental complications, as they do not occasion, or even aggravate, the mischief done to the medulla itself. Thus the ligaments, as in the case just related, may be torn through so as to allow of partial separation of contiguous vertebrae, or, as in Ollivier's or in Case 4, a vertebra may be fractured – but without any displacement of the broken fragments, or other sign by which it is possible during life to determine the exact amount of injury that has been inflicted on the parts external to the cord. In this respect injuries of the spine again closely resemble those of the head – their chief importance depending, not on the amount of injury to the containing, but on that inflicted upon the contained parts. In the spine just as in the head, it will sometimes be found after death from what appears to be, and in reality is, simple injury of the nervous centres, that the vertebral column in the one case, and the skull in the other, have suffered an amount of injury that was unsuspected during life; and which, though it may not in any way have determined to the fatality of the result, yet affords conclusive evidence of the violence to which the parts have been subjected, and the intensity of the disorganizing shock that they have suffered.

There is, however, this very essential difference between the spine and the head in these respects – that a simple fracture of the cranium may be of no moment except so far as the violence that has occasioned it may have influenced the brain. Whilst in the spine the case is not parallel; for as the vertebral column is the centre of support to the body, its influence in this respect will be lost when broken; even though the spinal cord may not have beeninjured by the edges of the fractured vertebras, but simply violently and fatally concussed by the same force that broke the spine itself.

Boyer had previously noticed the very interesting practical fact, that when the interspinous ligaments were ruptured in consequence of forcible flexion of the spine forwards, no fatal consequences usually ensue, the integrity of the parts being restored by rest. But that when the ligamenta subflava are torn through, and the arches separated, paraplegia and death ensue. This he attributes to stretching of the spinal cord. Sir C. Bell, however, with great acuteness, has pointed out the error of this explanation, and states that " it is the progress of inflammation to the spinal marrow, and not the pressure or the extension of it, which makes these cases of subluxation and breach of the tube fatal" (p. 149). There can be no doubt that this explanation is the correct one, and that when once the spinal canal is forcibly torn open, fatal inflammation will spread to the meninges and to the medulla itself.

Perhaps the most marked case on record of inflammatory softening of the cord consequent upon concussion of it, unattended with any injury to t'he osseous or ligamentous structures of the spine, is that which occurred in the practice of Dr. Hunter, of Edinburgh, and is related by Abercrombie. It is that of a man thirty-six years of age, who fell from the top of a wagon, a height of ten feet, into a pile of small stones, striking his back between the shoulders. He was immediately rendered paraplegic. When admitted into the Edinburgh Infirmary at the end of a month he was greatly emaciated: there was paralysis of motion, but not of sensation, in the lower extremities, retention of urine, involuntary liquid motions, deep-seated pain on pressure in the region of the third, fourth, and fifth dorsal vertebras. Three days after admission tetanic symptoms came on ; then more general spasms of the limbs and body, of which he died in forty-eight hours. On examination, after death there was no injury found to the spine itself. There was a high degree of vascularity of the pia mater of the cord in the dorsal region. There was most extensive softening of the body of the cord, affecting chiefly the anterior columns. "These were most remarkably softened throughout almost the whole course of the cord; in many places entirely diffluent; the posterior columns were also softened in many places, though in a much smaller degree" (p. 348).

3

SECTION 3

This case epitomizes so succinctly and clearly the symptoms and after-death appearances occurring in cases of inflammatory softening after uncomplicated concussion of the cord from severe and direct violence, that it needs neither comment nor addition.

The consideration of these subjects in connection with concussion of the spine, as the result of severe and direct violence, will pave the way for what I shall have to say in the next lecture about concussion of the spine as the result of slight, indirect, and less obvious injuries.

LECTURE THE THIED.

ON CONCUSSION OP THE SPINE FROM SLIGHT INJURY.

Concussion of the Spine from Slight Injuries – Railway Injuries Peculiar but not Special – Effects of Slight Blows on Spine, Case 5 – Concussion from Railway Injury, Case 6 – Concussion from Railway Injury, Case 7 – Concussion from Carriage Accident, Case 8 – Concussion from Falls – Long durations of Symptoms.

In the last lecture I directed your attention to the symptoms, effects, and pathological condition presented by cases of concussion of the spine, proceeding from the infliction of severe injury directly upon the vertebral column so as immediately and injuriously to influence the organization and the action of the delicate nervous structures included between it.

My object in the present lectures is to direct your attention to a class of cases in which the injury inflicted upon the back is either very slight in degree, or in which the blow, if more severe, has fallen upon some other part of the body than the spine, and in which, consequently, its influence upon the cord has been of a less direct and often of a less instantaneous character.

These cases are extremely interesting to the surgeon, for not only is the relation between the injury sustained and the symptoms developed less obvious than in the former case, but in consequence of the length of time that often intervenes between the occurrence of the accident and the production of the more serious symptoms, it becomes no easy matter to connect the two in the relation of cause and effect.

Symptoms indicative of concussion of the spine have of late years not unfrequently occurred, in consequence of injuries sustained in railway collisions, and have been very forcibly brought under the observation of surgeons in consequence of their having been the fertile sources of litigation; actions for damages for injuries alleged to have been sustained in railway collisions having become of such very frequent occurrence as now to constitute a very important part of medico-legal inquiry.

The symptoms arising from these accidents have been very variously interpreted by surgeons, some practitioners ignoring them entirely, believing that they exist only in the imagination of the patient, or, if admitting their existence, attributing them to other conditions of the nervous system than any that could arise from the alleged accident. And when their connection with, and dependence upon, an injury have been incontestably proved, no little discrepancy of opinion has arisen as to the ultimate result of the case, the permanence of the symptoms, and the curability or not of the patient.

I will endeavour in these Lectures to clear up these important and very intricate questions; and in doing so I shall direct your attention most particularly to the following points: –

1. The effect that may be produced on the spinal cord by slight blows when inflicted on the back or distant part of the body.

2. The length of time that may intervene between the alleged injury and the development of the symptoms.

3. The diagnosis of the symptoms of " Concussion of the Spine," from those arising from other morbid states of the nervous system.

4. The grounds on which to form a prognosis as to the probable result.

I shall illustrate these various points by selected cases, not only of persons who have been injured on railways, but in the ordinary accidents of civil life.

I wish particularly to direct your attention to the fact that there is in reality no difference whatever between the symptoms arising from a concussion of the spine received in a railway collision and those from a fall or ordinary accident – except perhaps in severity – and that it is consequently an error to look upon a certain class of symptoms as special to railway accidents. I cannot, indeed, too strongly impress upon you the fact that there is in reality nothing special in railway injuries, except in the severity

of the accident by which they are occasioned. They are peculiar in their severity, not different in their nature from injuries received in the other accidents of civil life.

There is no more real difference between that concussion of the spine which results from a railway collision and that which is the consequence of a fall from a horse or a scaffold, than there is between a compound and comminuted fracture of the leg occasioned by the grinding of a railway carriage over the limb and that resulting from the passage of the wheel of a street cab across it. In either case the injury arising from the railway accident will be essentially of the same nature as that which is otherwise occasioned, but it will probably be infinitely more severe and destructive in its effects, owing to the greater violence by which it has been occasioned. I intend to draw my illustrations, to some extent at least, from ordinary accidents, as in these the question of compensation in money for injury sustained is not mooted, and hence an element which is usually alleged to have a disquieting effect on the nervous system of the sufferer is eliminated from our consideration.

The consideration of the effects that may be produced on the spinal cord by *slight* blows, whether applied to the back or to a distant part of the body, is not altogether a matter of modern surgical study arising from the prevalence of railway accidents, but had, long antecedent to the introduction of modern means of locomotion, arrested the attention of observant practitioners.

Abercrombie, writing in 1829, says that chronic inflammations of the cord and its membranes "may supervene upon very slight injuries of the spine;" and further on he says, "Every injury of the spine should be considered as deserving of minute attention. The more immediate effect of anxiety in such cases is inflammatory action, which may be of an acute or chronic kind; and we have seen that it may advance in a very insidious manner even after injuries that were of so slight a kind that they attracted at the time little or no attention" (p. 381).

Nothing can be clearer and more positive than this statement. These remarks of Abercrombie's are confirmed by Ollivier, by Bell, and by other writers on such injuries.

The following cases will illustrate this point.

The first two are cases of concussion of the spine resulting from railway accidents, in which there were at the time slight marks of external injury. The others are very similar cases occurring from other accidents than those received on railways.

Case 5. – Mr. R., 35 years of age, a farmer and miller, of very active habits, accustomed to field sports, and much engaged in business, habitually in the enjoyment of good health, was *in* a railway collision that took place on Nov. 4, 1864. He received a blow upon his face which cut his upper lip on the left side, and was much and severely shaken. He did not lose consciousness, and was able shortly to proceed on his journey. On leaving the station to proceed to his own home, it was observed by a friend who drove him that he did not appear to recollect the road, with which he was familiar, having been in the daily habit of driving over it for years.

On reaching home, feeling bruised, shaken, and confused, he took to his bed, but did not feel sufficiently ill to seek medical advice until November 9, five days after the accident, when he sent to Mr. Yorke, of Staunton, who continued to attend him. But notwithstanding every attention from that gentleman, he progressively, but slowly got worse.

I saw Mr. R. for the first time on the 18th February, 1866, fifteen months after the occurrence of the accident, when I found him in the following state. His face was pallid, much lined, indicative of habitual suffering. He looked much older than his alleged age (36 years). He was sitting with his back to the light, and had the Venetian blinds drawn down so as to shade the room, the light being peculiarly distressing to him. His skin was cool. Tongue slightly furred, appetite moderate, digestion impaired. Pulse 104 to 106, weak and compressible. I understand from Mr. Yorke that it rarely fell below this, and often rose above it. He has not lost flesh, but all his friends say that he is quite an altered man.

He states that since the accident his memory has been bad – that he cannot recollect numbers – does not know the ages of his children, for instance – he cannot add up an ordinary sum correctly – he will add up the same set of figures if transposed differently. Before the accident he was considered to be a peculiarly good judge of the weights of beasts – since its occurrence he has lost all power of forming an opinion on this point. He has been quite unable to transact any business since the injury. Is troubled with frightful dreams. Starts and wakes up in terror, not knowing where he is. Has become irritable, and can neither bear light nor noise. He frowns habitually, so as to exclude the light from his eyes. He complains of stars, sparks, flashes of light and coloured spectra flaming and flashing before the eyes. He cannot read for more than two or three minutes at a time, the letters becoming confused, and the effort being painful to bear. On examining the state of the eyes, I find that vision is good in the right eye, but that this organ is over sensitive to light. Vision is nearly lost in the left eye, so much so that he cannot read large print with it.

His hearing is over sensitive with the right ear, dull on the left side. He cannot bear noises of any kind, more particularly if sudden ; they are peculiarly distressing to him. Even that of his children at play annoys him.

He complains of a numb sensation accompanied by tingling, burning sensations on the right side, in the right arm and leg, more particularly in the little and ring-fingers, and along the course of the ulnar nerve. The rest of the right hand feels numb. He makes no complaint of the left arm or leg. These sensations are worst in the morning.

He cannot stand or walk without the support of a stick, or by resting his hand on a piece of furniture. He can do so in this way on the left leg, but if he attempts to do so on the right foot the limb immediatly bends, and sinks as it were under him. His gait is very peculiar. He separates the feet so as to make a straddling movement, and brings one foot very slowly before the other. He advances the right foot less than the left, and does not raise the sole as far from the ground. The foot seems to come down too quickly. He does not drag with the toes, but does not raise the heel sufficiently, and is apt to catch it in walking in inequalities on the ground. Flexion and extension are more perfectly and rapidly performed with the left than the right foot.

The attitude of his body in walking is very peculiar: the back is stiff, the head fixed, and he looks straight forward without turning it to the one side or the other.

He has great difficulty in going up or down stairs, cannot do so without holding on by the banisters. The difficulty is greatest in going down stairs, and if he attempts this without support he falls or rolls over to the right side.

There is no appreciable difference in the size of the two legs, but the right feels colder than the left. The patient complains of the coldness of both legs and feet.

The spine had lost its natural flexibility, so that the patient kept the body perfectly straight, fixed, and immovable. He could not bend the body in any direction without suffering severe pain. This was complained of equally whether the patient bent forwards, backwards, or sideways. It was most severe on any attempt being made to twist the spine. He sits in a rigid and upright attitude.

There was considerable pain at the occipito atloid articulation, as also at that between the axis and atlas. If an attempt was made to bend the head forcibly forwards, or to rotate it, the patient suffered so severely that it became necessary to desist. When directed to look round, the patient turned the whole body.

Owing to the rigidity of his spine he could not stoo-p so as to pick anything off' the floor without going down on one knee.

On examining the spine by pressure and percussion, three tender spots were found; one in the upper cervical, the other in the middle dorsal, and the third in the lumbo-sacral region. There is pain both on superficial and on deep pressure at these spots. The pain is limited to the spine, and does not extend to the muscular structures on either side of it.

The power of retaining the urine is very materially diminished. He passes water four or five times in the night, and every second hour during the day. The urine is sub-acid.

The generative power, though impaired, is not lost. A remarkable circumstance has been noticed in this case by Mr. E.'s wife and his friends. It is that since the accident he is unable to judge correctly of the distance of objects in a *lateral* direction, though he appears to be able to do so when looking straight forward. Thus, when driving in the middle of a straight road he always imagines that the carriage is in danger of running into the ditch or hedge on the *near* side.

The opinion I gave was, that the patient had sustained an injury of the spinal cord, and that the base of the brain was also, to some extent, though probably secondarily, involved. That chronic subacute meningitis of the spine and base of the cranium had taken place. That it was not probable that he would ever completely recover, and that it was even doubtful whether, as the disease had up to the present time been progressive, it might not continue to be so, and terminate in incurable disorganization of the nervous centres. The patient was seen by Sir Charles Hardings and Mr. Garden, who took a similarly unfavourable view of his present state and probable future.

An action was brought at the spring assizes at Worcester, in 1866, against the company on whose line the patient had been injured. No surgical evidence was called for the company, the statement made by the plaintiffs medical advisers being accepted. The question of damages resolved itself, to a great extent, into one of loss of income and expense incurred. The jury awarded $5775.

Case 6. – Mr. J., 43 years of age, a wine-merchant, healthy and of active business habits, was in a railway collision on the 23d of August, 1864. He was suddenly dashed forwards and then, rebounded violently backwards.

When he extricated himself from the ruins of the carriage in which he had been travelling (a third-class one), he believed himself to be unhurt – suffering from no immediate effect of the shock he had sustained. He assisted his fellow-passengers, many of whom were much injured, and was thus actively engaged for two hours.

On his return home the same evening, he was greatly excited and very restless; he felt chilly, and his arms and legs tingled. He could not sleep that night.

On the following day he felt ill and shaken; could not attend to his business, and was lame from some slight contusions on his legs. He continued much in this state for several days, and was seen by Mr. Everett, of Worcester (to whom I am indebted for the early history of this case), on the 1st of September, eight or nine days after the accident. He was then much disturbed in health; his pulse was feeble, he looked anxious and depressed; he complained of violent pains in the head, confusion of thought, and loud noises in the ears and head. He also complained, but slightly, of pain in the back.

These symptoms continued for some time without improvement. He found more and more difficulty in walking, and his right ankle often gave way. This appeared to Mr. Everett to be owing to some spasmodic action of the muscles of the leg rather than to any weakness of the joint itself.

He now began to show more serious symptoms in connection with the nervous system. His memory became worse and confusion of ideas greater; he often called people and things by wrong names; addressed his wife as " sir."

The pains in the head became more violent, and assumed a paroxysmal character. There was acute sensibility to sound in, the right ear, deafness of the left. Vision of the right eye was rather dim.

This was his condition at the end of twelve weeks after the occurrence of the accident. The symptoms, though progressively assuming a more and more serious character, did not do so uninterruptedly, but, as Mr. Everett expresses it, were "undulatory," – sometimes better, sometimes worse; but yet at the expiration of any given time of a few weeks' duration, decidedly and persistently worse than at an earlier period.

Three months after the accident he began to complain, for the first time, of contractions of the muscles of the right arm and hand. His fingers became flexed, so that force was required to straighten them. Shortly afterwards the left arm became similarly affected. These contractions assumed an intermitting and spasmodic character, and occurred several times daily.

The pain in the back, which was but slightly complained of at first, now became more and more severe. It was more acute over the sixth to the tenth dorsal vertebra, both inclusive. Spasms of the diaphragm now came on occasionally, and distressed him much.

His gait was peculiar; beseemed to be uncertain where to set his feet, and he kept his head steadily fixed.

On February 1, 1865, five months after the accident, he complained, for the first time, of pain in the neck, greatly increased on moving the head.

During the whole of this period his digestion had been fairly good. He had gained flesh since the accident. There had been no loss of power over the sphincters, and his urine was normal and acid.

I saw this patient, in consultation with Mr. Garden and Mr. Everett, of Worcester, on March 8th, 1865, and found that the symptoms above detailed continued, and had somewhat increased in intensity since the last report.

Loss of memory, confusion of thought and ideas, utter incapacity for business, disturbed sleep, pains and noises in the head, partial deafness of the left, morbid sensibility of the right ear, irritability of the eyes, rendering light very painful – though vision had be- come imperfect in the right eye. Numbness, tingling sensation,

and formication in the right arm and leg, were the most prominent *subjective* symptoms.

He walked with a peculiar unsteady straddling gait; was obliged to feel with his right foot before planting it on the ground; did not raise the heel, but carried the foot flat, and let it fall suddenly; instead of putting it on the ground in the usual way; used a stick, or supported himself by the furniture.

He could stand for a moment on the left leg, but immediately fell over if he attempted to do so on the right.

His right arm and hand were numb; the little and ring-fingers contracted. He could not pick up a small object, as a pin, between his finger and thumb, nor could he write easily or legibly.

The spine was very tender at three points – in the upper cervical, in the middle dorsal, and in the lower lumbar regions. There was constant fixed aching pain in it in these situations. This pain was greatly increased on pressure; it was limited to the vertebral column, and did not extend beyond it.

Movement of any kind greatly increased the pain. If the head was raised by the hands and bent forward, or rotated, so as to influence the articulations between the occipital bone, the atlas, and the axis, the patient shrieked with the agony that was occasioned.

He could not bend the body either forwards, backwards, or sideways, the pain being so greatly increased in the dorsal and lumber regions by these movements. He consequently could not stoop.

The spine had entirely lost its normal flexibility. It was perfectly rigid, moved as a whole as if made of one bone. The patient could neither bend nor turn his head. Hence he could not look on the ground in walking to see where to place his feet; and when he wished to look round, he had to turn the whole body.

The pulse was feeble, about 98. Countenance pale, anxious, haggard. Tongue slightly coated. Digestive and other functions well performed. Urine clear and acid.

The case was tried at the spring Assizes at Worcester in 1865. The opinion expressed by Mr. Garden, Mr. Everett, and myself, 'amounted to this, that the patient was suffering from concussion of the spine, which had developed irritation or chronic inflammation of its membranes and of the cord, and that his recovery was very doubtful. The plaintiff recovered $6000 damages.

At this time (May, 1866), a year and nine months after theaccident, he is still an invalid, being so completely shattered in health that he has been obliged to winter in the southwest of England, and is quite unequal to attend to business of any kind.

Case 7. – The following case illustrates the fact that a train of symptoms of a most persistent nature, closely resembling those detailed in the preceding cases, may occur from other causes than railway accidents.

Captain N., 38 years of age, consulted me on October 27th, 1862. Looks careworn, pale, lined, and at least ten years older than his real age. He states that in November, 1854 – eight years previously, he had been thrown out of a pony-chaise, which was accidentally upset. At the time he hurt his right knee and bruised the right arm, but sustained no blow or evidence of injury on the head or back. He was much bruised and shaken at the time, but did not suffer any serious ill effects for several months after the accident, although during the whole of this period he felt ailing, and that he was in some way suffering from the injury he had sustained.

About six months after the accident he began to be troubled with the following train of symptoms, which have continued ever since: Confusion of thought; his memory was impaired; he had giddiness, especially on moving the head suddenly; his sight became impaired; he suffered from muscse volitantes; sparks and flashes of light; he could not continue to read beyond a few- minutes, partly because the letters ran into each other, partly because he could not concentrate his thoughts so as to fix his attention.

He now began to suffer from a feeling of numbness and a sensation of " pins and needles " in both hands, but more particularly the left, and chiefly in those parts supplied by the ulnar nerve.

He complained of the same sensations in the left leg and foot. He walked with difficulty, and with the legs somewhat apart, using a stick, or else supporting himself by holding on to pieces of furniture in the room as he passed them. He can stand on the right leg, but the left one immediately gives way under him. He walks with great difficulty up and down stairs, obliged to put both feet on the same step. The spine is tender on pressure and percussion in the lower cervical region and between the shoulders. It is stiff'; he cannot bend the back without pain, and cannot stoop without falling forward.

He has irritability of the bladder, passing water every second or third hour, and can only do so in a sitting position. He has completely lost all sexual power and desire. The urine is slightly acid. These symptoms have continued with varying intensity, since their commencement, about six months after the accident. He thinks they were most severe about a year after they began, and have somewhat improved since then. But he has never been free from them, or enjoyed a day's health, for the last seven and a half years, and never expects to do so.

This case closely resembles, in all its general features, and in many of its details, those that have just been related. It only differs in the symptoms being less intense, as would naturally be expected, from the accident that occasioned them being less severe than those which occur from railway collisions. The persistence of the symptoms for so lengthened a period as nearly eight years is significant of the long duration of the pernicious effects of these insidious injuries to the nervous system.

But the interminable duration of the most serious nervous phenomena, from comparatively slight injuries of the spine, receives additional illustration from the following case.

Case 8. – Miss B., 26 years of age, was brought to my house on the 11th April, 1866, by my friend Dr. Gibb. She looked moderately healthy, was of good constitution, with no discernible hereditary tendency to disease of any kind – was not anemic. The digestive and uterine functions were well performed. She has had no disease except that from which she now suffers, no convulsions or fits in childhood.

When about eighteen months old, she fell out of her cot and injured her cervical spine. From that time to the present she has suffered from a continuous and remarkable train of nervous phenomena. These were aggravated about the period of puberty, and at the age of 17 were still further increased in consequence of her falling over a stile backwards. She has never had hysteria in any of its ordinary forms, paralysis, epilepsy, or convulsive attacks of any kind.

On examining the spine, I find it straight and the body well formed. There is a distinct projection backwards of the spinous processes of the fifth and sixth cervical vertebra. She complains of a constant pressure and pain of a grating or grinding character in this region, as if the bones were in contact with one another. There is no evidence of abscess or of any distinct mischief in or around the tender vertebras, and nothing is to be observed with the laryngoscope at the anterior part of the cervical vertebras or pharynx. From this point a peculiar sense of uneasiness spreads itself over the whole of the body and limbs, producing nervous sensations of the most distressing character. These sensations, which consist of tingling and painful feelings, prevent her sitting still or lying down quietly for any length of time. She is better when in movement. She cannot sleep for more than an hour or two at a time, and is conscious of her sufferings through her sleep.

Her power of movement has never been impaired, the distress being confined to sensation, and not producing any disturbance of motion.

She can walk well under certain circumstances, can stand, and in fact scarcely ever sits; but cannot turn suddenly without becoming giddy, with the fear of falling.

She can walk well so long as there is anything near her. Thus she can walk along a street guided by the area railings; but when she comes to an open space, as a square or crossing, she is lost, and requires to be guided or she would fall. She cannot bear the sensation of having a space around her, and would then fall unless supported.

She has unceasing loud noises in her head, which she compares to "gravel-stones" rolling through it. They are so loud that she thinks that other people must hear them.

Her hearing is good.

Her sight is strong, but she sees the circulation of the blood in her own eyes, the corpuscles spinning round in convolutions, and often coloured. No perversion of smell or taste. The hands and feet always cold, even in summer.

She has been from first to last under the care of at least thirty medical men. Has had every variety of treatment adopted – a seton kept open in the neck and the clitoris excised; but so far from benefiting has slowly but steadily become worse, and her genera] health is now beginning to give way.

This lady, who is remarkably intelligent, gave a lengthened and minute history of her ailments, of which the above is a sketch. She referred all her morbid sensations to the seat of excurvation in the cervical vertebrae. At this point there had evidently existed disease leading to organic changes to which the remarkable train of general phenomena presented by this case were doubtless referable. If I were to hazard an opinion, it would be that some thickening of the meninges of the cord had probably taken place, the effect of which was to interfere with the sensory portions of the cord, rather than with the motor.

LECTURE THE FOURTH.

CONCUSSION OP THE SPINE FROM GENERAL SHOCK.

Concussion from General Shook – Case 9. Concussion from Shock to Feet – Case 10. Concussion from Railway Shock – Case 11. Concussion from Railway Shock – Case 12. Concussion from Railway Shock – Twists, Sprains, and Wrenches of the Spine – Case 13. Wrench of Spine – Case 14. Twist of the Spine – Effects of Twists and Wrenches of the Spine.

There is another class of cases of an extremely insidious and protracted character to which I wish to direct your attention, *viz.,* those cases in which the patient has received no blow or injury upon the head or spine, but in which the whole system has received a severe shake or shock, in consequence of which disease is developed in the spinal cord, perhaps eventually extending to the membranes of the brain. These cases, although necessarily more frequent in railway than in other injuries, yet occasionally occur as a consequence of ordinary accidents. I will first relate a case of this kind, and then direct your attention to the details of several instances that have fallen under my notice of similar phenomena occurring after railway accidents.

Case 9. – On the 17th November, 1861, I saw, in consultation with Dr. Strong, of Croydon, Mrs. B., 32 years of age. She states that in November, 1860, whilst going down-stairs, she accidentally stepped upon the side of a pail, and slipped forwards, bumping down three or . four stairs forcibly on her heels. She did not lose her footing, did not fall, and did not strike any part of the body or head. Of this she is quite certain. She felt nervous, faint, and skaken at the time, and was obliged to take some brandy. At the period of the occurrence of the accident, and up to that time, she had been a strong, healthy, and active woman. She was married, andthe mother of two children. She had never suffered from any disease of the nervous system, or from any serious complaint.

Two days after the trifling accident that has just been described, she was attacked with neuralgic pains in the right side of the head – apparently hemicrania. For this she was treated in the usual way, and did not feel it necessary to lay up. About a fortnight after the accident, she felt numbness and tingling conjoined in the right arm, hand, and leg, and also on the right side of the head, where the neuralgia had previously existed. The numbness after a time extended to the right half of the tongue.

When I saw her three months after the accident the numbness and tingling existed unchanged in these parts, and the left hand and arm had also begun to be affected. She felt a numb sensation in the little and ring-fingers, and slightly in the middle finger.

Although there is this numb sensation in the hands, and in the right leg, she has no impairment of motion. She can pick up a pin, untie a knot, and otherwise use the right hand, which is the one most affected, in ordinary small occupations. She can stand; walk fairly well.

I saw the patient again on the 13th April, four months after the accident. Notwith-standing the treatment that had been adopted (iron and strychnine), she was weaker, looked anaemic, and was rather worse, so far as the paralytic symptoms were concerned. She could no longer pick up so small an object as a pin, but can pick up a piece of money – a shilling for instance. The right hand and leg are still the worst, but the left limbs are more affected than they were. In the left hand the numbness has now affected the little, ring, and middle fingers, with the tip of the forefinger.

From this time to the present there has been a very slow increase in the symptoms, notwithstanding a great variety of treatment to which the patient has been subjected by the many different medical men whom she has seen. On examining her, on April 10,1866, about five and a half years after the accident, with Mr. Ay ling, her present medical attendant, she tells me that she feels that she is gradually, though very slowly, getting worse. She has an anxious, anaemic look. She totters in walking, so that in going about the room she supports herself by the chairs and tables. She could not in any way walk a quarter of a mile. She can stand unsupported on the left leg, but she immediately falls over if she attempts to do so on the right. The right hand and foot are much colder thanthe left. The paralysis of the hands continues much the same, but a marked change has taken place in the right hand in consequence of the contraction of all the fingers, but more especially of the little and ring-fingers. They have become rigid, and the flexor tendons stand out strongly. She can, consequently, scarcely use this hand. On testing the irritability of the muscles in the opposite limbs by galvanism, the contraction was almost *nil* in those of the right arm and hand. Much stronger, though not normally strong, on the left side.

She complains of confusion of thought and loss of memory; the senses are unimpaired. Appetite is bad, and digestion imperfect. Urine is acid. Can hold her water well.

In this case a very trivial accident occasioned a jar communicated to the feet, and evidently transmitted to the nervous centres, leading to impairment of innervation, and eventually to progressive and incurable paralysis.

Case 10. – M. H. I., a surgeon, 43 years of age, naturally a stout healthy man, of active professional habits, consulted me on February 22d, 1865. He states that on 9th October, 1864, he was in a railway collision, by which he was thrown forwards, but without any great violence. He received no blow on the back, head, or other part of the body. He was much frightened and shaken, but did not lose consciousness.

Beyond a general sensation of illness, he did not suffer much for the first three or four weeks after the accident, but he was not able to attend to his business; could not collect his thoughts sufficiently for the purpose.

About a month after the accident he began to suffer from pain across the loins. He could not walk without great fatigue. He lost strength and flesh, and his pulse became habitually much more frequent than natural, being about 98 to 100.

At the present time, four and a half months after the accident, he continues much in the same state ; is quite unfit for business, and has been obliged to relinquish practice; not owing to any mental incapacity, but entirely owing to his bodily infirmities. His mind is quite clear, and his senses perfect, though over-sensitive; loud and sudden noises and bright light being peculiarly distressing to him.

He complains chiefly of the spine. He suffers constant pain in the lower part of it, in the lower dorsal, and the lumbar regions. He compares the sensation there experienced to that of a wedge or plug of wood driven into the spinal canal. It is a mixed sensation of pain and distension. The spine generally is tender, and the pain in it is greatly increased by manipulation, pressure, and pur- cussion. It has lost its normal flexibility, moves as a whole, so that he cannot bend forwards or stoop. There is no pain in the cervical region, or on moving the head.

He complains of painful numbness and formications in the right, and occasionally down the left leg. The legs are stiff' and weak, especially the right one. He cannot stand unsupported on this for a moment. He walks in a slow and awkward manner – straddling – not able to place the feet together. If told to stand on his toes, he immediately falls forwards. He has lost control over the limbs, and does not know exactly where to place the feet. He has a frequent desire to pass water, suffers greatly from flatus, and has completely lost all sexual desire and power. The pulse was at 98; appetite bad; digestion impaired.

I saw this patient again, at Brighton, towards the end of April, seven months after the accident, in consultation with Mr. Curtis, and found that his condition had in no way improved; indeed, that in some respects, so far especially as power of movement was concerned, it had progressively become worse.

In this case the injury produced by the shock had evidently occasioned mischief within the lower portion of the spinal canal, leading to partial paraplegia. I believe this mischief to have been of a chronic inflammatory nature; the tenderness of the spine, the feeling of distension, the pain in movement, and the habitually high pulse, point in this direction. This case was settled out of court for $2500.

Case 11. – Mr. C. W. E., about 50 years of age, naturally a stout, very healthy man, weighing nearly seventeen stone, a widower, of very active habits, mentally and bodily, was in a railway collision on February 3d, 1865. He was violently shaken to and fro, but received no bruise or any sign whatever of external injury. He was necessarily much alarmed at the time, but was able to proceed on his journey to London, a distance of seventy or eighty miles. On his arrival in town he felt shaken and confused, but went about some business, and did not lay up until a day or two afterwards. He was then obliged to seek medical advice, and felt himself unable to attend to his business. He slowly got worse, and more out ofhealth. Was obliged to have change of air and scene, and gradually, but not uninterruptedly, continued to get worse, until I saw him on the 26th March, 1866, nearly fourteen months after the accident. During this long period he had been under the care of various medical men in different parts of the country, and had been most attentively and assiduously treated by Dr. Elkington, of Birmingham, and by several others, as Dr. Bell Fletcher, Dr. Gilchrist, Mr. Gamgee, Mr. Martin, &c. He had been most anxious to resume his business, which was of an important official character, and had made many attempts to do so, but invariably found himself quite unfit for it, and was most reluctantly constrained to relinquish it.

When I saw him at this time, he was in the following state: –

He has lost about twenty pounds in weight, is weak, unable to walk a quarter of a mile, or to attend to any business. His friends and family stated that he is, in all respects, "an altered man." His digestion is impaired, and his pulse is never below 96.

He complains of loss of memory, so that he is often obliged to break off in the midst of a sentence, not being able to complete it, or to recollect what he has commenced saying. His thoughts are confused, and he cannot concentrate his attention beyond a few minutes upon any one subject. If he attempts to read, he is obliged to lay aside the paper or book in a few minutes, as the letters become blurred and confused. If he tries to write, he often mis-spells the commonest words; but he has no difficulty about figures. He is troubled with horrible dreams, and wakes up frightened and confused.

His head is habitually hot, and often flushed. He complains of a dull confused sensation within it, and of loud noises which are constant.

The hearing of the right ear is very dull. He cannot hear the tick of an ordinary watch at a distance of six inches from it. The hearing of the left ear is normal, he can hear the tick at a distance of about twenty inches. Noises, especially of a loud, sudden, or clattering character, distress him greatly. He cannot bear the noise of his own children at play.

The vision of the left eye has been weak from childhood. That of the right, which has always been good, has become seriously impaired since the accident. He suffers from muscse volitantes, and sees a fixed line or bar, vertical in direction, across the field of vision. He complains also of flashes, stars, and coloured rings.

Light, even of ordinary day, is especially distressing to him. In fact, the eye is so irritable that he has an abhorrence of light. He habitually sits in a darkened room, and cannot bear to look at artificial light – as of gas, candles, or fire. This intolerance of light gives a peculiarly frowning expression to his countenance. He knits and depresses his brows in order to shade his eyes.

The senses of smell and taste seem to be somewhat perverted. He often thinks that he smells fetid odours which are not appreciable to others, and has lost his sense of taste to a great degree. He complains of a degree of numbness, and of "pins and needles" in the left arm and leg, also of pains in the left leg, and a feeling of tightness or constriction. All these symptoms are worst on first rising in the morning.

He walks with great difficulty, and seldom without the aid of a stick; whilst going about a room he supports himself by taking hold of the articles of furniture that come in his way. He does not bring his feet together – straddles in his gait – draws the left leg slowly behind the right – moves it stiffly and keeps the foot flat in walking, so that the heel catches the ground and the limb appears to drag. He has much difficulty in going up and down stairs, cannot do so without support.

He can stand on the right leg, but if he attempts to do so on the left, it immediately bends and gives way-under him, so that he would fall.

The spine is tender on pressure and on percussion of these points, *viz.,* at lower cervical, in middle dorsal, and in lumbar regions. The pain in these situations is increased on moving the body in any direction, but especially the antero-posterior. There is a degree of unnatural rigidity, of want of flexibility, about the spine, so that he cannot bend the body – he cannot stoop without falling forwards.

On testing the irritability of the muscles by galvanism, it was found to be very markedly less in the left than in the right leg.

The genito-urinary organs are not affected. The urine is acid, and the bladder neither atonic nor unduly irritable.

The opinion that I gave in this case was to the effect that the patient had suffered from concussion of the spine – that secondary inflammatory action of a chronic character had been set up in the meninges of the cord – that there was partial paralysis of theleft leg, probably dependent on structural disease of the cord itself – and that the presence of cerebral symptoms indicated the existence of an irritability of the brain and its membranes. The patient brought an action for damages at the Gloucester Spring Assizes, April, 1866, against the company on whose line he had been injured, and, notwithstanding powerful adverse medical testimony, recovered $3500 damages.

Case 12. – The following case presents some very remarkable and unusual nervous phenomena, resulting from railway shock, which I will briefly relate to you.

"*March* 1, 1865. Mr. D. is a man of healthy constitution and active habits, aged 33. He was travelling in an 'express' (third class, with divided compartment), and was seated with his back to the engine. When near Doncaster, the train going at about thirty miles an hour, ran into an engine standing on the line. He was thrown violently against the opposite side of the carriage, and then fell on the floor.

"*Immediate effects.* – There was a swelling the size of an egg over the sacrum, severe pain in the lower part of the spine, which, on arriving at Edinburgh the same day, had extended up the whole back and into the head, producing giddiness and dimness of sight. These, with tingling feelings in the limbs (particularly the left), great pain in the back, and tenderness to the touch, sickness in the mornings, and lameness, continued for the first fortnight.

"The *treatment* adopted consisted of blisters and hot fomentations to the spine.

"The patient seemed to improve, and the pain to move more between the shoulders after these applications.

"28th. He was seen by an eminent surgeon, who ordered him to go about as much as possible, but to avoid cold. The result of this advice was that he found the whole of the symptoms much increased with prostration and lameness.

"*April* 20th. Left for London, breaking journey for a week in Lancashire, greatly fatigued by journey. A discharge came on from the urethra, lameness much increased, could not advance the left leg in front of the right, and great prostration."

I saw him, in consultation with Mr. Hewer, May 1, 1865, when I received the above account from the patient. He was then suffering from many of the "subjective" phenomena which are common to persons who have incurred a serious shock to the system. But in addition to these, he presented the following somewhat peculiar and exceptional symptoms: –

1. An extreme difficulty in articulation, in the nature of a stammer or stutter of the most intense kind, so that it was extremely difficult to hold a continuous conversation with him. Although he had, previously to the accident, some impediment in his speech, this has been aggravated to the degree that has just been mentioned, so as to constitute the most intense stutter that I have ever heard in an adult.

2. A very peculiar condition of the spine and the muscles of the back.

The spine is rigid – has lost its natural flexibility to antero- posterior as well as to lateral movement.

There is an extreme degree of sensibility of the skin of the back, from the nape of the neck down to the loins. This sensibility extends for about four inches on either side of the spine. It is most intense between the shoulders.

This sensibility is both superficial and deep. The superficial or cutaneous sensibility is so marked, that on touching the skin lightly or on drawing the finger down it, the patient starts forwards as if he had been touched with a red-hot iron. There is also deep pain on pressure along the whole length of the spine, and on twisting or bending it in any direction.

Whenever the back is touched at these sensitive parts, the muscles are thrown into violent contraction so as to become rigid, and to be raised in strong relief, their outlines becoming clearly defined.

3. The patient's gait is most peculiar. He does not carry one leg before the other alternately in the ordinary manner of walking, but shuffles sideways, carrying the right leg in advance, and bringing up the left one after it by a series of short steps. He can alternate the action of the legs, but he cannot bring one leg in front of the other without twisting the whole body and turning, as on a pivot, on the leg that supports him. He cannot bend the thigh on the abdomen.

I saw this patient several times during the summer and autumn. In the early part of December, his condition was as nearly as possible the same as that which has been described in May, no change whatever in pain or in gait having taken place. There wasnot at this time, nor had there ever been, any signs of paralysis, but he complained of the sensation of a tight cord round the waist.

In addition to Mr. Hewer and myself, this patient was seen at different times by Sir W. Fergusson, Drs. Reynolds and Walshe. We all agreed that the patient was suffering from " concussion of the spine," and that his ultimate recovery was uncertain. Mr. D. brought an action against the railway company, which was tried at Guildhall, in December, 1865, and recovered $4750 damages.

Since the trial he has been continuously under my care, and I have seen him at intervals of about a month. He has been treated by perfect rest, lying on a Prone couch; by warm salt-water douches to the spine, for which purpose he has resided at Brighton, and by full doses of the bromide of potassium. Under this treatment he has considerably improved (May, 1866). The extreme sensibility of the back is materially lessened, and he can walk much better than he did. He also stammers less vehemently, but he still has considerable rigidity about the spine, can only walk with the aid of a stick, and retains that peculiar careworn, anxious, and aged look that is so very characteristic of those who have suffered from these injuries.

I shall now direct your attention to another very peculiar and interesting class of cases, those in which the spine has been violently twisted or strained, but not concussed or jarred.

Twists, Speains, or Wbenches Of The Spine, without fracture or dislocation of the vertebrae, may occur in a variety of ways.

Boyer relates a fatal case of this kind, occurring from an injury received in practising gymnastics. Sir A. Cooper gives an instance, to which I shall refer, of a fatal wrench of the spine from a rope catching a boy round the neck whilst swinging.

In two cases which I shall relate, the injury also arose from violence applied to the cervical spine; in one from a railway accident, in the other from a fall from a horse.

These wrenches of the spine are, from obvious reasons, most liable to occur in the more mobile parts of the vertebral column, as the neck and loins; less frequently in the dorsal region.

In railway collisions, when a person is violently and suddenly jolted from one side of the carriage to the other, the head is frequently forcibly thrown forwards and backwards, moving as it were by its own weight, the patient having momentarily lost control over the muscular structures of the neck. In such cases the patientcomplains of a severe straining, aching pain in the articulations between the head and the spine, and in the cervical spine itself. This pain closely resembles that met with in any joint after a severe wrench of its ligamentous structures, but is peculiarly distressing in the spine, owing to the extent to which fibrous tissue and ligament enter into the composition of the column. It is greatly increased by motion of any kind, and however slight, to and fro, and especially by rotation. The pains are greatly increased on pressure and on lifting up the head, so as to put the tissues on the stretch. In consequence of this, the patient keeps the neck and head immovable, rigid, looking straight forwards – neither turning to the right nor to the left. He cannot raise his head off a pillow without the assistance of his hand, or that of another person.

The lumbar spine is often strained in railway collisions, with or without similar injury to the cervical portion of the column, in consequence of the body being forcibly swayed backwards and forwards during the oscillation of the carriage on the receipt of a powerful shock. In such cases the same kind of pain is complained of. There is the same rigidly inflexible condition of the spine, with tenderness on external pressure, and great aggravation of suffering on any movement being impressed upon it, more particularly if the patient bends backwards. The patient is unable to stoop; in attempting to do so, he always goes down on one of his knees.

These strains of the ligamentous structures of the spinal column are not unfrequently associated with some of the most serious affections of the spinal cord that are met with in surgical practice as a consequence of injury.

They may of themselves prove most serious, or even fatal. Thus, in Case 13, we have an instance of loosening of the cervical portion of the spinal column to such an extent that the patient could not hold the head upright without artificial support.

In Case 14, we have an example of inflammatory swelling developing around the sprained part to such an extent as to compress the cord and spinal nerves, and thus lead to paralysis. And lastly, in Sir A. Cooper's case, we have an instance of a sprain of the spine terminating in death, and a description of the post-mortem appearances presented by this accident.

The *prognosis* will depend partly on the extent of the stretching of the muscular and ligamentous structures, partly on whetherthere is any inflammatory action excited in them which may extend to the interior of the spinal canal.

As a general rule, where muscular, tendinous and ligamentous structures have been violently stretched, as in an ordinary sprain, however severe, tliey recover themselves in the course of a few weeks, or at most within three or six months. If a joint, as the shoulder or ankle, continues to be weak and preternaturally mobile, in consequence of elongation of the ligaments, or weakness or atrophy of the muscles, beyond this period, it will, in all probability, never be so strong as it was before the accident.

The same holds good with the spine; and a vertebral column, which, as in Case 13, has been so weakened as to require artificial support, after a lapse of eleven months, in order to enable it to maintain the weight of the head, will not, in all probability, ever regain its normal strength and power of support.

One great prospective danger in strains of the spine is the possibility of the inflammation developed in the fibrous structures of the column extending to the meninges of the cord. This I have several times seen occur, and I believe that in Cases 6 and 11 this happened. We see that this is particularly apt to happen when the strain or twist occurs between the occiput and the atlas or axis. In these cases a rigid tenderness is gradually developed, which is most distressing and persisting and evidently of an inflammatory character.

Or, as in Case 13, the paralysis may remain incomplete, being confined to the nerves which are connected with that part of the spine which is the seat of the wrench, one or other of their roots either having suffered lesion, or the nervous cord itself having been injured in its passage through the intervertebral foramen.

Lastly, as in Sir A. Cooper's case, a twist of the spine may slowly and insidiously be followed by symptoms of complete paraplegia, and eventually by death from extravasation of blood into the vertebral canal.

Case 13. – Miss , a lady, 28 years of age, was involved in
the terrible catastrophe that occurred on the South Eastern Railway, at Staplehurst, on June 9, 1865, when in consequence of a bridge giving way a portion of a train was precipitated into a shallow stream. This lady lav for two hours and a half under a mass of broken carriages and debris of the bridge, another lady, a fellow-passenger, who had been killed, being stretched across her.

Miss was lying in such a position that she could not move.

Her head was forcibly twisted to the right side, and the neck bent forwards.

When extricated she was found to be a good deal cut about the head and face, and the left arm was extensively bruised, ecchymosed, and perfectly powerless.

Her neck had been so violently twisted or wrenched that for a
long time Miss - lost completely all power of supporting the
head, which she says felt loose. It used to fall on any side, as if the neck was broken, usually hanging with the chin resting on the breast.

Without going into an unnecessarily minute detail of all the distressing symptoms with which this young lady was affected, it suffices to say that she gradually recovered from all her general bodily sufferings, except these conditions, *viz.,* a weakened state of the neck, a loss of power in the left arm, and pain in the lower part of the back.

The neck had been so severely twisted and sprained that the ligamentous and muscular structures seemed to be loosened, so that in order to keep the bead in position she was obliged to wear a stiff collar lest the head should fall loosely from side to side. At first it had a special tendency to fall forwards; but after a time the tendency was in a backward direction. When lying on her back she had no power whatever to raise her head, and was obliged to do so with her right hand put under it so as to support it. If she wished to get up when in bed, for instance, she was obliged to assume a most distressing action, being compelled to roll over on to her face, and then, pressing the forehead against the pillow, get upon her knees.

There was no pain in the cervical spine, nor could any irregularity of the vertebras be detected. There was no pain in forcibly moving the head on the atlas, or rotating this bone on the axis. The looseness appeared to be in the lower part of the cervical spine.

The left arm had at first and for many weeks been completely powerless, all sensation as well as power of motion in it having been lost. Sensation gradually and slowly returned. But the whole of the nerves of the brachial plexus appeared to be partially paralyzed, so far as motor influence was concerned. The circumflex, the musculo spiral, the median and the ulnar were all affectedto such a degree as to occasion great loss of power to the muscles they respectively supplied. Thus she could not use the deltoid so as to raise the arm to the top of the head. She could not pick up a pin or even a quill between the thumb and forefinger. She could not hold a book. The power of grasping with the left hand and fingers was infinitely less than with the ripht, and there was some rigid contraction of the little and ring-fingers. The muscles of the left hand and of the ball of the thumb were wasted.

This crippled and partially paralyzed state of the left arm was a most serious and distressing inconvenience to the patient. Before the accident she had been an intrepid rider, a skilful driver, and an accomplished musician, playing much on the harp and piano. All these pursuits were necessarily completely put a stop to, and from being remarkable for her courage she had become so nervous as scarcely to be able to drive in a carriage.

Mr. Tapson had most skilfully and assiduously attended this very distressing case almost from the time of the accident, and the patient had occasionally had the advantage of Mr. Holmes Coote's advice. When I saw Miss in consultation with these gentlemen on April 20, 1866, ten and a half months after the accident, they told me that the condition of the neck had certainly, though very slowly, improved, but that the state of the left arm, which was such as has just been described, had undergone no change for several months.

The pain in the lower part of the back had increased during the last two months. There was no disturbance of the mind, and no sign of cerebral irritation. The bodily health generally was fairly good – as much so as could be expected under the altered circumstances of life that this accident had in so melancholy a manner entailed on this young lady.

The state of the cervical spine in this case was most remarkable. It was movable at its lower part in all directions as if it were attached to a universal joint, or had a ball-and-socket articulation, the weight of the head carrying it in all directions. It was almost impossible to conceive so great a degree of mobility existing without dislocation – but there was certainly neither luxation nor fracture, the vertebraa being apparently loosened from one another in their ligamentous connections and their muscular supports, so that the weight of the head was too great for the weakened spine to carry.

This loosening was most marked in the lower cervical region, and did not exist between the atlas and the occiput. It was clearly the direct result of the violent and long-continued wrench to which this part of the spine had been subjected.

The paralysis was confined to the left arm, no other part of the body having been affected by it. At first the paralysis was complete, the arm being perfectly powerless and sensation being quite lost. After a time sensation returned, but motion was still very imperfect, and no improvement had taken place in this respect for several months. As the nerves of the whole of the brachial plexus were implicated, and apparently to the same degree, it was'difficult to account for this in any other way than by an injury inflicted upon them at their origin from the cord, or on their exit through the vertebral column. I think it most probable that this latter injury was the1 real cause of nervous weakness to the left arm, for the spine had been wrenched in the lower cervical region, in that part, in fact, which corresponds to the origin of the brachial plexus, and there was not at the time of my visit, nor did there appear to have been at any previous period, any disturbance in the functions of the spinal cord as a whole; the paralysis being entirely and absolutely localized to the parts supplied by the left brachial plexus, implicating these only so far as motor power was concerned, and affecting no other portion of the nervous system.

This lady brought an action for damages against the railway company at Guildhall in the spring of 1866. But as she had sustained no pecuniary loss by the accident, she was only awarded the wretched "compensation" of $1350. Mental sufferings, bodily pain, and disability, and complete annihilation of the prospects of a life, weigh lightly in the scales of justice, which are only made to kick the beam by the burden of the actual money loss entailed by the accident.

Case 14. – The following case, which I have seen several times in consultation with Dr. Russell Reynolds, under whose immediate care the patient was, and to whom I am indebted for its early history, affords an excellent illustration of some of the effects that may result from a severe twist or wrench of the spine.

Mr. G., about 23 years of age, a strong, well-formed, healthy, young man, thrown from his horse on December 12, 1865. He fell on the back of his head, on soft ground, and rolled over. He got up immediately after the fall and walked to his house, a distance of about one hundred yards. He had no cerebral disturbance whatever, being neither insensible, delirious, concussed, nor sick. The head was twisted to the left side, and he felt pain in the neck He kept his bed in consequence of this pain in the neck till January 1st, 1866, and his room for a week longer. At this time he tried to write, but found great difficulty in controlling his right arm. He managed, however, to do so, and did write a letter. He was under surgical treatment in the country, and was not considered to have paralysis, as he could use his arms well for all ordinary purposes, and could walk without difficulty.

Towards the end of January, nearly six weeks after the accident, symptoms of paralysis very gradually and slowly began to develop themselves. The right arm became cold, numb, and was affected by creeping sensations. His right leg became weak, unequal to the support of the body, and he dragged his right foot.

He came to town on February 21st, when he was seen for the first time by Dr. Reynolds, who reports that at this period the paralysis of the right arm had become complete, and that of the right foot was partial, the patient walking with a drag of the foot. His limbs gave way under him, so that he had occasionally fallen. He had no pain in any part of the body; his mind was clear, but he was very restless. V

On the 27th February, whilst stooping, he fell in his bedroom, struggled much, and was unable to rise. He was found, after a time, lying partly under his bed. On the following day it was found that the left side was partially paralyzed, the right side continuing in the condition already described. There was now considerable swelling and tenderness on the left side of the neck and about the third and fourth cervical vertebra). He was seen shortly after this by Dr. Jenner, in consultation with Dr. Reynolds, and was ordered complete rest, with large doses of iodide of potass.

I saw him on March 3d, in consultation with Dr. Reynolds. I found him lying on his back in bed. The mind quite clear; spirits good. No appearance of anxiety or distress in the countenance; in fact I was much struck by the happy, cheerful expression of his countenance under the melancholy circumstances in which he was placed.

I found his condition much as has been described. There was complete paralysis of the right arm, partial of the right leg. The left arm was also partially paralyzed, and the left leg slightly so. He was unable to stand. There was no affection of the bladder or of the sphincter ani. The skin was hot and perspiring; the pulse quick; urine acid.

He could not raise his head off the pillow, and lay quite flat on his back. On being raised up in the sitting posture, it was necessary to support his head with the hands; and when he was seated upright, he held the head firmly fixed, the spine being kept perfectly rigid. He was quite unable to turn or move the head.

The back of the neck was swollen, especially on the left side, and was tender on pressure. The swelling was less than it had been. The cervical vertebras felt as if they were somewhat twisted, so that the head inclined towards the right side. It was doubtful whether this was really so. The patient continued the iodide of potass; and a gutta-percha case, extending from the top of his head to the pelvis, and embracing the shoulders and back of the chest, was moulded on him, so as to keep the head and spine motionless. He was ordered to lie on his back and not to move.

I saw the patient several times with Dr. Reynolds, and we-were gratified to find that a steady improvement was taking place. On March 27th he had completely lost all symptoms of paralysis on the left side of the body ; the right leg had recovered its power, and the paralytic sympims had almost entirely disappeared from the right arm. He could raise it, grasp'with his hand, and in fact use it for the ordinary purposes of life. He could stand, though in a somewhat unsteady way. This seemed rather owing to his having kept the recumbent position for so long a time than to any loss of nervous power in the legs.

The swelling of the neck had entirely subsided, and the cervical spine was straight, but it was rigid, and he could not turn the head. The support was habitually worn, and gave him great comfort.

This case is remarkable in several of its points. In the first place, the fact that the paralysis did not begin to show itself until several weeks – nearly six – had elapsed from the time of the accident is a matter of the greatest consequence in reference to these injuries. Then, again, the fact that although the brain was throughout unaffected, and the injury purely spinal, the paralysis was of a hemiplegic and not a paraplegic character, is also not without import. And lastly, the gradual subsidence of the very threatening symptoms with which the patient was affected, and the disappearance of the paralysis of'the limbs in the inverse order to that in which it developed itself in them, should be observed.

That wrenches or twists of the spine may slowly develop paralytic symptoms, and may be attended eventually by a fatal result, is well illustrated by a case recorded by Sir Astley Cooper as occurring in the practice of Mr. Heaviside. It is briefly as follows: A lad, 12 years old, whilst swinging in a heavy wooden swing, was caught under the chin by a rope, so that his head and the whole of the cervical vertebra? were violently strained. As the line immediately slipped off', he thought no more of it. For some months after the occurrence he felt no pain or inconvenience, but it was observed that he was less active than usual, and did not join in the games of his schoolfellows. At that time it was found that he was really weaker than before the occurrence. He suffered from pains in the head and in the back of the neck, the muscles of which part were stiff, indurated, and very tender to external pressure. Movement of the head in any direction gave rise to pain, and there was diminution in voluntary power of motion in his limbs.

Eleven months after the accident the complaint and the paralytic affection of the limbs were gradually getting much worse, added to which he felt a most vehement and burning pain in the small of his back. His symptoms gradually became worse, difficulty of breathing set in, and he died exactly twelve months after the accident.

On examination after death the whole contents of the head were found to be perfectly healthy. There was no fracture or other sign of injury to the spine, but "the theca vertebralis was found overflowing with blood which was effused between the theca and the inclosing canals of bone. The effusion, extended from the first vertebra of the neck to the second vertebra of the back, both included."-1

This case is a most valuable one. It illustrates one of the important points in that last described, *viz.,* the very slow, gradual, and progressive development of paralysis in these injuries of the spine. And as it was attended by a fatal issue and the opportunity of a *post-mortem* examination, it also proves that this slow and progressive development of paralysis after an interval of " some months" may be associated with extensive and serious lesion

1 Sir A. Cooper, Fractures and Dislocations, 8vo. ed., p. 530. within the spinal canal, with the effusion, in fact, of a large quantity of blood upon the membranes of the cord, – the very condition that has already been shown (p. 38) to be the common accompaniment of many fatal cases of so-called "concussion of the spine."

Each of these three cases of twist of the spine is typical of a special group of these injuries. In the first-case we have sudden and immediate paralysis of one arm produced by the wrench to which that portion of the spine that gives exit to the nerves supplying that limb had been subjected.

In the second case we have paralysis, resulting after an interval of some weeks, as a consequence of the pressure of the secondary inflammatory effusions that had been slowly produced by tbe injury to the spine and its contents, – that paralysis disappearing as these effusions were absorbed.

In the third case we have an instance of death resulting in twelve months after a wrench of the spine by the effects of hemorrhage into the spinal canal.

LECTURE THE FIFTH.

Period at which Symptoms begin to develop – Length of Time that often elapses – Concussion not associated with other Injury – Nature of Changes produced by Concussion – Early Symptoms of Railway Concussion – Detail of Symptoms of Railway Concussion – Symptoms of Railway Concussion – Interval between Accident and Symptoms – Pathology of Railway Concussion – Mr. Gore's Case.

One of the most remarkable circumstances connected with injuries of the spine is, the disproportion that exists between the apparently trifling accident that the patient has sustained, and the real and serious mischief that has occurred. Not only do symptoms of concussion of the spine of the most serious, progressive, and persistent character, often develop themselves after what are apparently slight injuries, but frequently when there is no sign whatever of external injury. This is well exemplified in Case 9, the patient having been partially paralyzed simply by slipping down a few- stairs on her heels. The shake or jar that is inflicted on the spine when a person jumping from a height of a few feet comes to theground suddenly and heavily on his heels or in sitting posture, has been well known to surgeons as not an uncommon cause of spinal weakness and debility. It is the same in railway accidents; the shock to which the patient is subjected in them being often followed by a train of slowly-progressive symptoms indicative of concussion and subsequent irritation and inflammation of the cord and its membranes.

But I may not only say that sudden shocks applied to the body are liable to be followed by the train of evil consequences that we are now discussing. I may even go further, and say that these symptoms of spinal concussion seldom occur when a serious injury has been inflicted on one of the limbs, unless the spine itself has at the same time been severely and directly struck. A person who by any of the accidents of civil life meets with an injury 'by which one of the limbs is fractured or is dislocated, necessarily sustains a very severe shock, but it is the rarest thing possible to find that the spinal cord or the brain has been injuriously influenced by this shock that has been impressed on the body. It would appear as if the violence of the shock expended itself in the production of the fracture or the dislocation, and that a jar of the more delicate nervous structures is thus avoided. I may give a familiar illustration of this from an injury to a watch by falling on the ground. A watchmaker once told me that if the glass was broken, the works were rarely damaged; if the glass escapes unbroken, the jar of the fall will usually be found to have stopped the movement.

How these jars, shakes, shocks, or concussions of the spinal cord . directly influence its action I cannot say with certainty. We do not know how it is that when a magnet is struck a heavy blow with a hammer, the magnetic force is jarred, shaken, or concussed out of the horse-shoe. But we know that it is so, and that the iron has lost its magnetic power. So, if the spine is badly jarred, shaken, or concussed by a blow or shock of any kind communicated to the body, we find that the nervous force is to a certain extent shaken out of the man, and that he has in some way lost nervous power. What immediate change, if any, has taken place in the nervous structure to occasion that effect, we no more know than what change happens to a magnet when struck. But we know that a change has taken place in the action of thenervous system just as we do in the action of the iron by the change that is induced in the loss of its magnetic force.

But whatever may be the nature of the primary change that is produced in the spinal cord by a concussion, the secondary effects are clearly of an inflammatory character, and are identical with those phenomena that have been described by Ollivier, Abercrombie, and others, as dependent on chronic meningitis of the cord, and subacute myelitis.

One of the most remarkable phenomena attendant upon this class of cases is, that at the time of the occurrence of the injury the sufferer is usually quite unconscious that any serious accident has happened to him. He feels that he has been violently jolted and shaken, he is perhaps somewhat giddy and confused, but he finds no bones broken, merely some superficial bruises or cuts on the head or legs, perhaps even no evidence whatever of external injury. He congratulates himself upon his escape from the imminent peril to which he has been exposed. He becomes unusually calm and self-possessed; assists his less fortunate fellow-sufferers occupies himself perhaps actively in this way for several hours, and then proceeds on his journey.

When he reaches his home, the effects of the injury that he has sustained begin to manifest themselves. A revulsion of feeling takes place. He bursts into tears, becomes unusually talkative, and is excited. He cannot sleep, or, if he does, he wakes up suddenly with a vague sense of alarm. The next day he complains of feeling shaken or bruised all over, as if he had been beaten, or had violently strained -himself by exertion of an unusual kind. This stiff and strained feeling chiefly affects the muscles of the neck and loins, sometimes extending to those of the shoulders and thighs. After a time, which varies much in different cases, from a day or two to a week or more, he finds that he is unfit for exertion and unable to attend to business. He now lays up, and perhaps for the first time seeks surgical assistance.

This is a general sketch of the early history of most of these cases of "concussion of the spine" from railway accidents. The details necessarily vary much in different cases.

There is great variation in the period at which the more serious, persistent, and positive symptoms of spinal lesion begin to develop themselves. In some cases they do so immediately after the occurrence of the injury, in others not until several weeks, I mightperhaps even say months, had elapsed. But during the whole of this interval, whether it be of short or of long duration, it will be observed that the sufferer's condition, mentally and bodily, has undergone a change. -His friends remark, and he feels, that "he is not the man he was." He has lost bodily energy, mental capacity, business aptitude. He looks ill and worn; oftan becomes irritable and easily fatigued. He still believes that he has sustained no serious or permanent hurt, tries to return to his business, finds that he cannot apply himself to it, takes rest, seeks change of air and scene, undergoes medical treatment of various kinds, but finds all of no avail. His symptoms become progressively more and more confirmed, and at last he resigns himself to the conviction that he has sustained a more serious bodily injury than he had at first believed, and one that has, in some way or other, broken down his nervous power, and has wrought the change of converting a man of mental energy and of active business habits into a valetudinarian, utterly unable to attend to the ordinary duties of life.

The condition in which a patient will be at this or a later period of his sufferings, will be found detailed in several of the cases that have been related, especially in Cases 5 and 6.

It may, however, throw additional light on this subject, if we analyze the symptoms, and arrange them in the order in which they will present themselves on making a surgical examination of such a patient, bearing this important fact in mind, however, that although all and every one of these symptoms may present themselves in any given case, yet that they are by no means all necessarily present in any one case. Indeed this usually happens, and we generally find that whilst some symptoms assume great prominence, others are proportionally dwarfed, or, indeed, completely absent.

The *countenance* is usually pallid, lined, and has a peculiarly careworn, anxious expression;. the patient generally looking much older than he really is or than he did before the accident. I have seen one instance of flushing of face. This was marked in Case 11.

The *memory* is defective. This defect of memory shows itself in vaious ways; thus, Case 2 said that he could not recollect a message unless he wrote it down; Case 6 forgot some common words and misspelt others; Case 5 lost command over figures; he could not add up a few figures, and had also lost, in a great degree, thefaculty of judging of weight, and of distance in a lateral direction; he forgot dates, the ages of his children, &c.

The *thoughts* are -confused. The patient will sometimes, as in Case 11, break ofl' in the middle of a sentence, unable to finish it; he cannot concentrate his ideas so as to carry out a connected line of argument; he attempts to read, but is obliged to lay aside the book or paper after a few minutes' attempt at perusal.

All *business aptitude* is lost, partly as a consequence of impairment of memory, partly of confusion of thought and inability to concentrate ideas for a sufficient length of time.

The *temper* often becomes changed for the worse, the patient being fretful, irritable, and in some way – difficult perhaps to define, but easily appreciated by those around him – altered in character.

The *sleep* is disturbed, restless, and broken. He wakes up in sudden alarm; dreams much; the dreams are distressing and horrible.

The *head* is usually of its natural temperature, but sometimes hot, as in Case 11. The patient complains of various uneasy sensations in it; of pain, tension, weight, or throbbing; of giddiness; of a confused or strained feeling in it. Frequently loud and incessant noises, described as roaring, rushing, ringing, singing, sawing, rumbling, or thundering. These noises vary in intensity at different periods of the day, but if once they occur, are never entirely absent, and are a source of great distress and disquietude to the patient.

The *organs of special sense* usually become more or less seriously affected. They become sometimes over sensitive and irritable, or are impaired in their perceptions, and at others perverted in their sensations. In many cases we find a combination of all those conditions in the same organ..

Vision is usually afi'ected in various ways and in very different degrees. In some cases, though rarely, there is double vision and perhaps slight strabismus. In others an alteration in the focal length, so that the patient has to use glasses, or to change those he has previously worn. The patient cannot read for more than a few minutes, the letters running into one another. More commonly, muscse volitantes and spectra, rings, stars, flashes, sparks – white, coloured, or flame-like – are complained of. This happened in Cases 5, 6, and 11. The eyes often become over sensitive to light, so that the patient habitually sits in a shaded or darkenedroom, turns his back to the window, and cannot bear unshaded gas- or lamp-light. This intolerance of light may amount to positive photophobia. It gives rise to a habitually contracted state of the brows, so as to exclude light as much as possible from the eyes- One or both eyes may be thus affected. Sometimes one eye only is intolerant of light. This intolerance of light may be associated with dimness and imperfection of sight. Perhaps vision is normal in one eye, but impaired seriously in the other. The circulation in the bottom of the eye is visible to some patients.

The hearing may be variously affected. Not only does the patient commonly complain of the noises in the head and ears that have already been described, but the ears, like the eyes, may be over sensitive or too dull.' One ear is frequently over sensitive whilst the other is less acute than it was before the accident. The relative sensibility of the ears may readily be measured by the distance at which the tick of a watch may be heard. Loud and sudden noises are particularly distressing to these patients. The fall of a tray, the rattle of a carriage, the noise of children at play, are all sources of pain and of irritation.

Taste and *smell* are sometimes, but more rarely, perverted. Case 11 complained of occasional fetid smells, which were not perceptible to any one else.

The *sense of touch* is impaired. The patient cannot pick up a pin, cannot button his dress, cannot feel the difference between different textures, as cloth and velvet. He loses the sense of *weight,* cannot tell whether a sovereign or a shilling is balanced on his finger. *Speech* is rarely affected. Case 12 stammered somewhat before the accident, but after it his speech became a most painful and an indescribably confused stutter that it was almost impossible to comprehend. The same phenomenon was observed in the Count de Lordat's case, p. 24. But it is certainly rare.

The *attitude* of these patients is usually peculiar. It is stiff and unbending. They hold themselves very erect, usually walk straight forwards, as if afraid or unable to turn to either side. The movements of the head or trunk, or both, do not possess their natural freedom. There may be pain or difficulty in moving the head in the antero-posterior direction, or in rotating it, or all movements may be attended by so much pain and difficulty that the patient is afraid to attempt them, and hence keeps the head in its attitude of immobility.

The movements of the trunk are often equally restrained, especially in the lumbar region. Flexion forwards, backwards, or sideways, is painful, difficult, and may be impossible; flexion backwards is usually most complained of.

If the patient is desired to stoop and pick anything off the ground, he will not be able to do so in the usual way, but bends down on the knee and so reaches the ground.

If he is laid horizontally and told to raise himself up without the use of his hands, he will be unable to do it.

The *state of the spine* will be found to be the real cause of all these symptoms.

On examining it by pressure, by percussion, or by the application of the hot sponge, it will be founfl that it is painful, and that its sensibility is exalted at one, two, or three points. These are usually the upper cervical, the middle dorsal, and the lumbar regions. The exact vertebras that are affected vary necessarily in different cases, but the exalted sensibility always includes two, and usually three, at each of these points. It is in consequence of the pain that is occasioned by any movement of the trunk in the way of flexion or rotation, that the spine loses its natural suppleness, and that the vertebral column moves as a whole, as if cut out of one solid piece, instead of with the flexibility that its various component parts naturally impress upon its motions.

The movements of the head upon the upper cervical vertebrae are variously affected. In some cases the head moves freely in all directions, without pain or stiffness, these conditions existing in the lower and middle, rather than in the upper, cervical vertebrae. In other cases, again, the greatest agony is induced if the surgeon takes the head between his hands and bends it forwards or rotates it, the articulations between the occipital bone, the atlas, and the axis, being evidently in a state of inflammatory irritation. This happened in a very marked manner in Cases 5 and 6; and in both these it is interesting to observe that distinct evidences of cerebral irritation had been superadded to those of the more ordinary spinal mischief.

The pain is usually confined to the vertebral column, and does not extend beyond the transverse processes. But in some instances, as in Case 12, the pain extended widely over the back on both sides, more on the left than on the right, and seemed to correspond with the distribution of the posterior branches of the dorsal nerves. lathese cases, from the musculo-cutaneous distribution of these nerves, the pain is superficial and cutaneous as well as deeply seated in the spine.

The muscles of the back are usually unaffected, but in some cases where the muscular branches of the dorsal nerves are affected, as in Case 12, they may be found to be very irritable and spasmodically contracted, so that their outlines are very distinct and marked.

The *gait* of the patient is remarkable and characteristic. He walks more or less unsteadily, generally uses a stick, or, if deprived . of that, is apt to lay his hand on any article of furniture that is near to him, with the view of steadying himself.

He keeps his feet somewhat apart, so as to increase the basis of support, and consequently walks in a straddling manner.

As one leg is often weaker than the other, he totters somewhat, raises one foot but slightly off the ground, so that the heel is apt to touch. He seldom drags the toe, but walking flat-footed as it were on one side, the heel drags. This peculiar straddling, tottering, unsteady gait, with the spine rigid, the head erect, and looking straight forwards, gives the patient the aspect of a man who walks blindfolded.

The patient cannot generally stand equally well on either foot. One leg usually immediately gives way under him if he attempts to stand on it.

He often cannot raise himself on his toes, or stand on them, without immediately tottering forwards.

His power of walking is always very limited; it seldom exceeds half a mile or a mile at the utmost.

He cannot ride, even if much in the habit of doing so before the accident.

There is usually considerable difBculty in going up and down stairs – more difficulty in going down than up. The patient is obliged to support himself by holding on to the banisters, and often brings both feet together on the same step.

A sensation as of a cord tied round the waist, with occasional spasm of the diaphragm, giving rise to a catch in the breathing, or hiccup, is sometimes met with, and is very distressing when it does occur.

The *nervous power of the limbs* will -be found to be variously modified, and will generally be so to very different degrees in the different limbs. Sometimes one limb only is affected, at others the armand leg on one side, or both legs only, or the arm and both legs, or all four limbs, are the seat of uneasy sensations. There is the greatest possible variety in these respects, dependent of course entirely upon the degree and extent of the lesion that has been inflicted upon or induced in the spinal cord.

Sensation only may be affected, or it may be normal, and motion may be impaired ; or both may be aft'ected to an equal, or one to a greater and the other to a less, degree. And these conditions may happen in one or more limbs. Thus sensation and motion may be seriously impaired in one limb, or sensation in one and motion in another. The paralysis is seldom complete. It may become so in the more advanced stages after a lapse of several years, but for the first year or two it is (except in cases of direct and severe violence) almost always partial. It is sometimes incompletely recovered from, especially so far as sensation is concerned.

The *loss of motor power* is especially marked in the legs, and more often in the extensor than in the flexor muscles. The extensor of the great toe is especially apt to suffer. The hand and arm are less frequently the seat of loss of motor power than the leg and foot; but the muscle of the ball of the thumb, or the flexors of the fingers, may be so affected.

The loss of motor power in the foot and leg is best tested by the application of the galvanic current, so as to compare the irritability of the same muscles of the opposite limbs. The value of the electric test is, that it is not under the influence of the patient's will, and that a very true estimate can thus be made of the loss of contractility in any given set of muscles.

The loss of motor power in the hand is best tested by the force of the patient's grasp. This may be roughly estimated by telling him to squeeze the surgeon's fingers, first with one hand arid then the other, or more accurately by means of the dynamometer, which shows on an index the precise amount of pressure that a person exercises in grasping.

It is in consequence of the diminution of motor power in the legs that those peculiarities of gait which have just been described are met with, and they are most marked when the amount of loss is unequal in the two limbs. The sphincters are very rarely affected in the cases now under consideration. Sometimes there is increased frequency of micturition, but I have rarely met with retention of 'urine or cases requiring the continued use of the catheter; norhave I observed in any case that the contractility of the sphincter ani had been so far impaired as to lead to involuntary escape of flatus or of feces.

Modification or diminution of sensation in the limbs is one of the most marked phenomena in these cases.

In many instances the sensibility is a good deal augmented, especially in the earlier stages. The patient complains of shooting pains down the limbs, like stabs, darts, or electrical shocks. The surface of the skin is sometimes over-sensitive in places on the back (as in Case 12), or in various parts of the limbs, hot, burning sensations are experienced in it. ft. fter a time these sensations give place to various others, which are very differently described by patients. Tinglings, a feeling of "pins and needles," a heavy sensation as if the limb was asleep, creeping sensations down the back and along the nerves, and formications, are all commonly complained of. These sensations are often confined to one nerve in a limb, as the ulnar, for instance, or the musculo-spiral.

Numbness, more or less complete, may exist independently of, or be associated with, all these various modifications of sensation with pain, tingling, or creeping sensations. Its extent will vary greatly; it may be confined to a part of a limb, may influence the whole of it, or may extend to several; its degree and extent are best tested by Brown-Sdquard's instrument.

Coldness of one of the extremities, dependent upon actual loss of nervous power, and defective nutrition, is often perceptible to the touch, and may actually be established by the thermometer; but in many cases it is found that the sensation of coldness is far greater to the patient than it is to the surgeon's hand, and not unfrequently no appreciable difference in the temperature of two limbs can be determined by the most delicate clinical thermometer, although the patient experiences a very distinct and distressing sense of coldness in one of the limbs.

The condition of the limbs as to size, and the state of their muscles, will vary greatly.

In some cases of complete paraplegia, which has lasted for years, as in Case 3, it has been remarked that no diminution whatever had taken place in the size of the limbs. This was also the case in Case 2, where the paralysis was partial. It is evident, therefore, that loss of size in a limb that is more or less completely paralyzed is not the simple consequence of the disuse of the muscles, or it would always occur. But it must arise from some modification of innervation, influencing the nutrition of the limb, independently of the loss of its muscular activity.

In most cases, however, where the paralytic condition has been of some duration, the size of the limb dwindles; and on accurate measurement it will be found to be somewhat smaller in circumference than its fellow on the opposite side.

The state of the muscles as to firmness will also vary. Most commonly when a limb dwindles the muscles become soft, and the inter-muscular spaces more distinct. Occasionally in advanced cases a certain degree of contmction and of rigidity in particular muscles sets in. Thus the flexors of the little and ring fingers, the extensors of the great toe, the deltoid or the muscles of the calf, may all become the seats of more or less rigidity and contractions.

The *body* itself generally loses weight; and a loss of weight, when the patient is rendered inactive by a semi-paralyzed state, and takes a fair quantity of good food, which he digests sufficiently well, is undoubtedly a very important and a very serious sign, and may usually be taken to be indicative of progressive disease in the nervous system.

When the progress of the disease has been arrested, though the patient may be permanently paralyzed, we often see a considerable increase of size and weight take place. This is a phenomenon of such common occurrence in ordinary cases of paralysis from disease of the brain, that I need do no more than mention that it is also of not unfrequent occurrence in those forms that proceed from injury, whether of the cord or brain.

The condition of the *genito-urinary* organs is seldom much deranged in the cases under consideration, as there is usually no paralysis of the sphincters. Neither retention of urine nor incontinence of flatus and feces occurs. Sometimes, as in Case 5, irritability of the bladder is a prominent symptom. The urine generally retains its acidity, sometimes markedly, at others but very slightly so. As there is no retention, it does not become alkaline, ammoniacal, or otherwise offensive.

The sexual desire and power are usually greatly impaired, and often entirely lost. Not invariably so, however. The wife of Case 5 miscarried twice during the twelve-month succeeding her husband's accident. I have never heard priapism complained of.

The pulse varies in frequency at different periods. In the earlystages it is usually slow; in the more advanced it is quick, near to or above 100. It is always feeble.

The order of the progressive development of the various symptoms that have just been detailed is a matter of great interest in these cases, and each separate symptom comes on very gradually and insidiously. It usually extends over a lengthened period.

In the early stages, the chief complaint is a sensation of lassitude, weariness, and inability for mental and physical exertion. Then come the pains, tinglings, and numbness of the limbs; next the fixed pain and rigidity of the spine; then the mental confusion and signs of cerebral disturbance, and the affection of the organs of sense; the loss of motor power, and the peculiarity of gait.

The period of the supervention of these symptoms after the occurrence of the injury will greatly vary. Most commonly after the first and immediate effects of the accident have passed off there is a period of comparative ease, and of remission of the symptoms, during which the patient imagines that he will speedily regain his health and strength. This period may last for many weeks, possibly for two or three months. At this time there will be considerable fluctuation in the patient's state. So long as he is at rest, he will feel tolerably well; but any attempt at ordinary exertion of body or mind brings back all the feelings or indications of nervous prostration and irritation so characteristic of these injuries; and to these will gradually be superadded those more serious symptoms that have already been fully detailed, which evidently proceed from a chronic disease of the cord and its membranes. After a lapse of several months – from three to six – the patient will find that he is slowly but steadily becoming worse, and he then, perhaps for the first time, becomes aware of the serious and deep-seated injury that his nervous system has sustained.

Although there is often this long interval between the time of the occurrence of the accident and the supervention of the more distressing symptoms, and the conviction of the serious nature of the injury that has been sustained, it will be found, on close inquiry, *that there has never been an interval of complete restoration to health.* There have been remissions, but no complete and perfect intermission in the symptoms. The patient has thought himself and has felt himself much better at one period than he was at another, so much so that he has been tempted to try to return to his usual occupation, but he has never felt himself well, and hasimmediately relapsed to a worse state than before when lie has attempted to do work of any kind.

It is by this chain of symptoms, which, though fluctuating in intensity, is yet continuous and unbroken, that the injury sustained, and the illness subsequently developed, can be linked together in the relation of cause and effect.

Having thus described the various symptoms that may arise from these shocks to and concussions of the spine, let us now briefly inquire into the pathological conditions that lead to and that are the direct causes of these phenomena.

I have already pointed out and discussed at some length, at p. 37 *et seq.,* the pathological conditions that are found within the spinal canal in those cases of paralysis, more or less complete, that result from direct and violent blows upon the back without fracture or dislocation of the bones entering into the formation of the vertebral column, and we have seen that in these cases the signs of spinal lesion are referable to extravasation of blood in various parts within the spinal canal, to rupture of the membranes of the cord, to inflammatory effusions, or to softening and disorganization of the cord itself.

In those cases in which the shock to the system has been general and unconnected with any local and direct implication of the spinal column by external violence, and where the symptoms, as just detailed, are less those of paralysis than of disordered nervous action, the pathological states on which these symptoms are dependent are of a more chronic and less directly obvious character than those above mentioned. They doubtless consist mainly of chronic and subacute inflammatory action in the spinal membranes, and in chronic myelitis, with those changes in the structure of the cord that are the inevitable consequences of a long-continued chronic inflammatory condition developed by it.

The only case on record with which I am acquainted, in which a *post-mortem* examination has been made of the spinal cord of a person who had actually died from the remote effects of concussion of the spine from a railway collision, is one that has very recently been related, and the parts exhibited to the Pathological Society by Dr. Lockhart Clarke. The patient, who had been under the care of Mr. Gore, of Bath, by whom the preparation was furnished, was a middle-aged man of active business habits. He had been ina railway collision, and, without any sign of external injury, fracture, dislocation, wound, or bruise, began to manifest the usual nervous symptoms. He gradually, but very slowly, became partially paralyzed in the lower extremities, and died three years and a half after the accident.

Mr. Gore has most kindly furnished me with the following particulars of the case. On the occurrence of the collision the patient walked from the train to the station close at hand. He had received no external sign of injury – no contusions or wounds, but he complained of a pain in his back. Being most unwilling to give in, he made every effort to get about in his business, and did so for a short time after the accident, though with much distress. Numbness and a want of power in the muscles of the lower limbs gradually but steadily increasing, he soon became disabled. There was great sensitiveness to external impressions, so that a shock against a table or chair caused great distress. As the patient was not under Mr. Gore's care from the first, and as he only saw the case for the first time about a year after the accident, and then at intervals up to the time of death, he has not been able to inform me of the precise time when the paralytic symptoms appeared, but he says that this was certainly within less than a year of the time of the occurrence of the accident. In the latter part of his illness some weakness of the upper extremities became apparent, so that if the patient was off his guard a cup or glass would, slip from his fingers. There was no paralysis of the sphincter of the bladder until about eighteen months before his death, when the urine became pale and alkaline, with muco-purulent deposits. In this case the symptoms were not so severe as usual, there was no very marked tenderness or rigidity of the spine, nor were there any convulsive movements.

On examination after death, traces of chronic inflammation were found in the arachnoid and the cortical substance of the brain. The spinal meninges were greatly congested, and exudative matter had been deposited upon the surface of the cord. The cord itself was much narrowed in its anterior-posterior diameter in the cervico- dorsal region. The narrowing was owing to absorption of the posterior columns. These had not only to a great extent disappeared, but the remains were of a dark brownish colour, and had undergone important structural changes. This case is of remarkable interest and practical value, as affording evidence of the changes that takeplace in the cord under the influence of " concussion of the spine' from a railway accident. Evidences of chronic meningitis – cerebral as well as spinal – of chronic myelitis, with subsequent atrophy, and other organic changes dependent on mal-nutrition of the affected portion of the cord being manifest.

It is well known to pathologists that two distinct forms of chronic subacute in-flammation may affect the contents of the spinal canal as the results of injury or of idiopathic disease, *viz.,* inflammation of the membranes, and inflammation of the cord itself.

In spinal meningitis the usual signs of inflammatory action in the form of vascular-ization of the membranes is met with. The meningo-rachidian veins are turgid with blood, and the vessels of the pia-mater will be found much injected, sometimes in patches, at others uniformly so. Serous fluid, reddened and clear, or opaque from'the admixture of lymph, may be found largely effused in the cavity of the arachnoid.

Ollivier1 states that one of the most constant signs of chronic spinal meningitis is adhesion between the serous lamina that invests the dura mater and that which corresponds to the spinal pia- mater. This he says he has often observed, and especially in that form of the disease which is developed as the result of a lesion of the vertebras. He has also seen rough cartilaginous (fibroid?) lamina? developed in the arachnoid. Lymph also of a puriform appearance has often been found under the arachnoid, between it and the pia-mater.

In distinguishing the various pathological appearances presented by fatal cases of chronic spinal meningitis, Ollivier makes the very important practical remark – the truth of which is fully carried out by a consideration of the cases related in Lectures 2 and 3 – that spinal meningitis rarely exists without there being at the same time a more or less extensive inflammation of the cerebral meninges, and hence, he says, arises the difficulty of determining with precision the symptoms that are special to inflammation of the membranes of the spinal cord.

When myelitis occurs, the inflammation attacking the substance of the cord itself, the most usual pathological condition met with is softening of its substance, with more or less disorganization ofits tissue. This softening of the cord as a consequence of its inflammation may, according to Ollivier, occupy very varying extents of its tissue. Sometimes the whole thickness of the cord is affected at one point, sometimes one of the lateral halves in a vertical direction is affected; at other times it is most marked in or wholly confined to its anterior or its posterior aspect, or the gray central portion may be more affected than the circumferential part. Then, again, these changes of structure may be limited to one part only, – to the cervical, the dorsal, or the lumbar. It is very rare indeed that the whole length of the cord is affected. The most common seat of the inflammatory softening is the lumbar region; next in order of frequency the cervical. In very chronic cases of myelitis, the whole of the nervous substance disappears, and nothing but connective tissue is left behind at the part affected.

' Vol. ii. p. 237.

Ollivier makes the important observation, that when myelitis is consecutive to meningitis of the cord, the inflammatory softening may be confined to the white substance.

But though softening is the ordinary change that takes place in a cord that has been the seat of chronic inflammation, yet sometimes the nervous substance becomes indurated, increased in bulk, more solid than natural, and of a dull white colour, like boiled white of egg. This induration of the cord may coexist with spinal meningitis, with congestion, and increased vascularization of the membranes. The case of the Count de Lordat (p. 24) is an instance of this induration and enlargement of the substance of the cord, and others of a similar nature are recorded by Portal, Ollivier, and Abercrombie.

It is important to observe, that although spinal meningitis and myelitis are occasionally met with distinct and separate from each other, yet that they most frequently coexist. When existing together, and even arising from the same cause, they may be associated with each other in very varying degrees. In some cases the symptoms of meningitis, in others those of myelitis, being most marked, and after death the characteristic appearances presenting a prominence corresponding to that assumed by their effects during life.

I have given but a very brief sketch of the pathological appearances that are usually met with in spinal meningitis and in. myelitis, as it is not my intention in these lectures to occupy yourattention with an elaborate inquiry into the pathology of these affections, but rather to consider them in their surgical relations.

I wish now to direct your attention to the symptoms that are admitted by all writers on diseases of the nervous system to be connected with and dependent upon the pathological conditions that I have just detailed to you, and to direct your attention to a comparison between these symptoms and those that are described in the various cases that I have detailed to you as characteristic of " concussion of the spine" from slight injuries and general shocks to the body.

The symptoms that I have detailed at pp. 74 to 83, arrange themselves in three groups : –

1st. The cerebral symptoms.

2d. The spinal symptoms.

3d. Those referable to the limbs.

In comparing the symptoms of " concussion of the spine " arising from railway and other accidents, as detailed in the cases I'have related to you, with those that are given to and accepted by the profession as dependent on spinal meningitis and myelitis arising from other causes, I shall confine the comparison of my cases to those related by Abercrombie and Ollivier. And I do this for two reasons, first, because the works of these writers on diseases of the spinal cord are universally received as the most graphic and classical on the subject of which they treat in this country and in France; and, secondly, because their descriptions were given to the world before the railway era, and consequently could in no way have been influenced by accidents occurring as a consequence of modern modes of locomotion.

1. With respect to the cerebral symptoms. It will be observed that in most of the cases that I have related, there was more or less cerebral disturbance or irritation, as indicated by headache, confusion of thought, loss of memory, disturbance of the organs of sense, irritability of the eyes and ears, &c.; – symptoms, in fact, referable to subacute cerebral meningitis and arachnitis.

On this point the statement of Ollivier is most precise and positive. He says that it is rare to find inflammation of the spinal membranes limited to the vertebral canal. That we see at the same time a more or less intense cerebral meningitis. In the cases that he relates of spinal meningitis, he makes frequent referenceto these cerebral symptoms – states that they often complicate the case so as to render the diagnosis difficult, especially in the early stages. In the *post-mortem* appearances that he details of patients who have died of spinal meningitis, he describes the morbid conditions met with in the cranium, indicative of increased vascularity and inflammation of the arachnoid. This complication of cerebral with spinal meningitis is nothing more than we should expect as a simple consequence of inflammation running along a continuous membrane. In both the fatal cases of meningitis of the spine recorded by Abercrombie, evidences of intracranial mischief are described.

2. The spinal symptoms that occurred in the cases of " concussion of the spine" which I have related, consisted briefly in pain at one or more points of the spine, greatly increased on pressure, and on movement of any kind, so as to occasion extreme rigidity of the vertebral column.

Ollivier says that one of the most characteristic signs of spinal meningitis is pain in the spine, which is most intense opposite the seat of inflammation. This pain is greatly increased by movement of any kind, so that the patient fearing the slightest displacement of the spine, preserves it in an absolute state of quiescence. This pain is usually accompanied by muscular rigidity. It remits, sometimes being much more severe than at others, and occasionally even disappears entirely. According to some observers, the pain of spinal meningitis is increased by pressure. But the correctness of this observation is doubted by Ollivier, who says that in chronic myelitis there is a painful spot in the spine where the pain is increased on pressure, and he looks upon this as indicative of inflammation of the cord rather than of the membranes.

3. The third group of symptoms dependent on concussion of the spine are those referable to the limbs. They have been described at pp. 81 – 83, and may briefly be stated to consist in painful sensations along the course of the nerves, followed by more or less numbness, tingling, and creeping; some loss of motor power affecting one or more of the limbs, and giving rise to peculiarity and unsteadiness of gait. No paralysis of the sphincters.

These are the very symptoms that are given by Ollivier andothers as characteristic of spinal meningitis, but more particularly of myelitis.

In spinal meningitis, says Ollivier, there is increased sensibility in different parts of the limbs, extending along the course of the nerves, and augmented by the most superficial pressure. These pains are often at first mistaken for rheumatism. There is often, also more or less contraction of the muscles.

In myelitis the sensibility is at first augmented, but after a time becomes lessened, and gives way to various uneasy sensations in the limbs, such as formications, a feeling as if the limb was asleep (engourdissement). These sensations are first experienced in the fingers and toes, and thence extend upwards along the limbs.

These sensations are most complained of in the morning soon after leaving bed. They intermit at times, fluctuating in intensity, and in the early stages are lessened after exercise, when the patient feels better and stronger for a time, but these attempts are followed by an aggravation of the symptoms. Some degree of paralysis of movement, of loss of motor power, occurs in certain sets of muscles – or in one limb. Thus the lower limbs may be singly or successively affected before the upper extremities, or *vice versd.* Occasionally this loss of power assumes a hemiplegic form. All this will vary according to the seat and the extent of the myelitis.

There is usually constipation in consequence of loss of power in the lower bowel. It is very rare that the bladder is early affected, the patient having voluntary control over that organ until the most advanced stages of the disease, towards the close of life, when the softening of the cord is complete.

Ollivier remarks, that in chronic myelitis patients often complain of a sensation as of a cord tied tightly round the body.

The gait (demarche) of patients affected with chronic myelitis is peculiar. The foot is raised with difficulty, the toes are sometimes depressed and at others they are raised, and the heel drags in walking. The body is kept erect and carried somewhat backwards.

If we take any one symptom that enters into the composition of these various groups, we shall find that it is more or less common to various forms of disease of the nervous system. But if we compare the groups of symptoms that have just been detailed, their progressive development and indefinite continuance, with those which are described by Ollivier and other writers of acknowledged authority on diseases of the nervous system, as characteristic of spinal meningitis and myelitis, we shall find that they mostly correspond with one another in every particular – so closely, indeed, as to leave no doubt that the whole train of nervous phenomena arising from shakes and jars of or blows on the body, and described at pp. 74 to 83 as characteristic of so-called "concussion of the spine," are in reality due to chronic inflammation of the spinal membranes and cord. The variation in different cases being referable partly to whether meningitis or myelitis predominates, and in a great measure to the exact situation and extent of the intra-spinal inflammation, and to the degree to which its resulting structural changes may have developed themselves in the membranes or cord.

LECTURE THE SIXTH.

DIAGNOSIS, PROGNOSIS, TREATMENT, OF CONCUSSION OP THE SPINE.

Diagnosis from Cerebral Concussion – From Rheumatism – From Hysteria – Prognosis of Concussion of the Spine – What is meant by Recovery – Probability of Recovery – Period of Fatal Termination – Treatment – Importance of Rest – Counter Irritation – Medical Treatment.

From the account that has just been given of the symptoms that may gradually develop themselves after concussion of the spine, I need say little about the diagnosis of this injury from other forms of cerebro-spinal disease. There are, however, three morbid states for one or other of which I have known it to be confounded, and from which it is necessary to diagnose it. These are, 1. The secondary consequences of cerebral concussion; 2. Eheumatism ; and 3. Hysteria.

1. *From the secondary effects of cerebral concussion* it is not difficult to diagnose the consequences of concussion of the spine, in those cases in which the mischief is limited to the vertebral column. The tenderness and rigidity of the spine, the pain on pressing upon or on moving it in any direction, and the absence of any distinct lesion about the head, will sufficiently mark the precise situation of the injury.

The two conditions of cerebral and spinal concussion often coexist primarily. The shock that jars injuriously one portion of the nervous system, very commonly produces a corresponding eS'ect on the whole of it, on brain as well as on cord; and, as has been fully pointed out in various parts of these lectures, the secondary inflammations of the spine, which follow the concussion, even when that is primarily limited to the vertebral column and its contents, have a tendency to extend along the continuous fibrous and serous membranes to the interior of the cranium, and thus to give rise to symptoms of cerebral irritation.

2. From *Rheumatism* the diagnosis may not always be easy, especially in the earlier stages of the disease, when the concussion of the spine and the consecutive meningitis have developed pain along the course of the nerves, and increased cutaneous sensibility at points. By attention, however, to the history of the case, the slow but gradually progressive character of the symptoms of spinal concussion, the absence of all fixed pain except at one or more points in the back, the cerebral complications, the gradual occurrence of loss of sensibility, of tinglings and formications, the slow supervention of impairment or loss of motor power in certain sets of muscles, – symptoms that do not occur in rheumatism, – the diagnosis will be rendered comparatively easy ; the more so when we observe that in spinal concussion there is never any concomitant articular inflammation, and that although the urine may continue acid, it does not usually present evidences of a superabundance of lithates.

3. *Hysteria* is the disease for which I have more frequently seen concussion of the spine, followed by meningo-myelitis, mistaken, and it certainly has always appeared extraordinary to me that so great an error of diagnosis could so easily be made.

Hysteria, whether in its emotional or its local form, is a disease of women rather than of men, of the younger rather than of the middle- aged and old, of people of an excitable, imaginative, or emotional disposition rather than of hard-headed, active, practical men of business. It is a disease that runs no definite or progressive course, that assumes no permanence of action, that is ever varying in the intensity, in the degree, and in the nature of its symptoms; that is marked by excessive and violent outbreaks of an emotional character, or by severe exacerbations of its local symptoms, but that is equally characterized by long-continued and complete intermissions of its various phenomena.

Does this in any way resemble what we see in "concussion of the spine," or in the consecutive meningo-myelitis? In those cases in which a man advanced in life, of energetic business habits, of great mental activity and vigour, in no way subject to gusty fits of emotion, or to local nervous disquietudes of any kind, – a man, in fact, active in mind, accustomed to self-control,. addicted to business, and healthy in body, suddenly, and for the first time in his life, after the infliction of a severe shock to the system, finds himself affected by a train of symptoms indicative of serious and deep- seated injury to the nervous system, – is it reasonable to say that such a man has suddenly become "hysterical," like a love-sick girl ? Or is this terra not rather employed merely to cloak a want of precise knowledge as to the real pathological state that has given rise to the alteration that is perceptible to the most casual observer in the mental state and bodily condition of the patient ? To me, I confess, the sight of a man of forty-five, rendered " hysterical," not for a few hours or days even, by some sudden and overwhelming calamity that may for the time break down his mental vigour, but permanently so for months or years, would be a novel and a melancholy phenomenon, and is one that I have neither seen described by any writer with whose works I am acquainted, nor Witnessed in a hospital experience of twenty-five years; and could such a condition actually be induced, it would certainly be to my mind an evidence of the most serious and disorganizing disease of the nervous system.

But, in reality, there can be but little difficulty in establishing the diagnosis between chronic meningo-myelitis and hysteria. The persistence of the symptoms, their slow development, their progressive increase in severity notwithstanding occasional fluctuations and intermissions in intensity, the invariable presence of more or less paralysis of sensation, or of motion, or both, will easily enable the surgeon to judge of the true nature of the case. That mental emotion is occasionally manifested by an unfortunate individual who has been seriously injured by an accident which tends to shake his whole nervous system, can scarcely be matter of surprise, the more so when, as commonly happens in these cases, he finds himself progressively and steadily deteriorating in health and strength, and sees in the future the gloomy prospect of a shattered constitution, of impaired mental vigour, and of loss of bodily activity; of the necessity of abandoning those occupations in whichhis life had been usefully spent, and on the continuance of which, probably, the support of himself and his family is dependent. That such an unhappy sufferer should occasionally be unnerved and give way to mental emotion is natural enough. It certainly appears to me that the term " hysteria," elastic as it is, can scarcely, with any regard to truth or justice, be strained so far as to embrace those feelings that naturally spring from the contemplation of so gloomy a prospect as this ; and even if it be considered applicable to his mental state, it can in no way be looked upon as the cause of those bodily sufferings and disabilities which constitute the most important and serious part of his disease, and which have no analogy in development or progress with the ordinary physical phenomena of hysteria.

The prognosis of " concussion of the spine" and that of the consecutive meningo-myelitis is a question of extreme interest in a medico-legal point of view, and is one that is often involved in no little difficulty.

The prognosis requires to be made with regard, first, to the life, and, secondly, to the health of the patient. So far as life is concerned, it is only in those cases of severe and direct blows upon the spine, in which intra-spinal hemorrhage to a considerable extent has occurred (Case 4), or in which the cord or its membranes have been ruptured, that a speedily fatal termination may be feared.

In some of the cases of concussion of the spine, followed by chronic inflammation of the membranes and of the cord itself, death may eventually supervene after several, perhaps three or four, years of an increasingly progressive breaking down of the general health, and the slow extension of the paralytic symptoms. I have heard of several instances in which concussion of the spine has thus proved fatal some years after the occurrence of the accident. Mr. Gore, of Bath, who has had considerable experience in these injuries, writes to me in reference to the case related p. 84, that this is the third fatal case of which he has had more or less personal knowledge, the time from the injury to the occurrence of death varying from two and a half to five years.

In these cases, as in the one related at p. 84, the fatal result is the direct consequence of the structural changes that take place in the cord and its membranes. Indeed, this one case proves in the clearest and most incontestable manner the possibility of deathoccurring after a lapse of several years, from the progressive increase of those symptoms, which are dependent upon disease of the nervous system from concussion of the spine occurring from railway accidents, and attended by the usual symptoms of such injuries; the fatal termination being gradually induced by the slow and . progressive structural changes which take place in the cord. This case establishes the fact beyond doubt that such a fatal termination is by no means impossible after an interval of several years, in cases of concussion of the spine in which deep- seated structural changes have developed in the cord.

The probability of such a melancholy occurrence is greatly increased if, after a year or two have elapsed from the time of the occurrence of the accident, the symptoms of chronic meningo- myelitis either continue to be gradually progressive, or, after an interval of quiescence, suddenly assume increased activity.

In fact, it is the excitation of this very form of disease, *viz.,* chronic inflammation of the spinal cord and its membranes, that constitutes the great danger in these injuries of the spine. When it has once gone on to the development of atrophy, softening, or other structural changes of the substance of the cord itself, complete recovery is impossible, and, ultimately, death is not improbable.

Ollivier states as the result of his experience, that although persons affected with chronic myelitis may live for fifteen or twenty years, yet that they more commonly perish within four years. This opinion as to the probable future of patients unfortunately affected by this distressing disease is perhaps too gloomy, so far as the fatal result is concerned, but it is an evidence of the very serious view that a man of such large experience in the diseases of the cord took of the probable issue of a case of chronic inflammation of that structure, and it is doubtless explicable by the fact that Ollivier's experience has necessarily been chiefly drawn from idiopathic or constitutional affections of that portion of the nervous system ; and these may justly be considered to be more frequently fatal than those forms of the disease that arise from accident to an otherwise healthy man not predisposed to such affections.

Ollivier takes an equally unfavourable view of the ultimate result of spinal meningitis, and probably for the same reason. He says:1 "Is spinal meningitis susceptible of cure? All-observers agree in stating that death is the inevitable result." He qualifies this statement, however, by saying that he has found in one case after death from other disease, old thickening of the membranes of the cord, and that Frank relates another in which a fatal termination did not occur. The occurrence of convulsive movements is a most unfavourable sign. They indicate the existence of chronic myelitis, and are usually associated with deep disorganization of the structure of the cord. They are of a most painful character, and are apt to be excited by movements and shocks of the body, even of a very slight character. I have never known a patient recover who has been afflicted by them, progressive paralysis developing itself, and the case ultimately proving fatal. Mr. Gore, of Bath, informs me that he is acquainted with two cases which proved fatal at long periods of time after the accident, in both of which this symptom was present. One of these, a very healthy lad of nineteen, was injured on October 29, 1863, and died May 11,1866. He suffered from convulsive attacks, with extreme pain in the spine, till the latter end of 1864, then the convulsions ceased, but the aching, wringing spinal pain continued; and his health broke down completely. Phthisis, to which there was no hereditary tendency, developed in the following spring, and he eventually died of that disease two years and a half after the injury.

From all this it is certain that concussion of the spine may prove fatal; first, at an early period by the severity of the direct injury (Case 4); secondly, at a more remote date by the occurrence of inflammation of the cord and its membranes (Ollivier); and, thirdly, after a lapse of several years by the slow and progressive development of structural changes in the cord and its membranes (Mr. Gore's Case, p. 84).

But though death may not occur, is recovery certain ? Is there no mid-state between a fatal result, proximate or remote, and the absolute and complete recovery of the patient ?

What is meant by the " recovery of the patient ?" When you are asked, " In your opinion will this patient ever recover ?" what are you to understand by that question ? Is it meant whether there will be a mitigation of the symptoms – an amelioration of

Vol. ii. p. 294.

health to some, perhaps even a considerable, extent – an indefinite prolongation of life, so that with care, by the avoidance of mental exertion and bodily fatigue of all kinds, the patient may drag on a semi-valetudinarian existence for fifteen or twenty years? Is this the meaning of the question ? No, certainly not. If that question has any definite meaning, it is whether the patient will in time completely and entirely lose all the effects of the injury he has sustained – whether in all respects, mentally and bodily, he will be restored to that state of intellectual vigour and of corporeal activity that he enjoyed before the occurrence of the accident – whether, in fact, he will ever again possess the same force and clearness of intellect, the same aptitude for business, the same perfection of his senses, the same physical energy and endurance, the same nerve, that he did up to the moment of his receiving the concussion of his spine.

In considering the question of recovery after concussion of the spine, we have to look to two points, first, the recovery from the primary and direct effects of the injury, and, secondly, from the secondary and remote consequences of it.

There can be no doubt that recovery, entire and complete, may occur in a case of concussion of the spine when the symptoms have not gone beyond the primary stage, when no inflammatory action of the cord or its membranes has been developed, and more particularly when the patient is young and healthy in constitution. This last condition indeed is a most important one. A young man of healthy organization is not only less likely to suffer from a severe shock to the system from a fall or railway injury than one more advanced in life, but, if he does suffer, his chance of ultimate recovery will be greater, provided always that no secondary and organic lesions have developed themselves.

I believe that such recovery is more likely to ensue if the primary and direct symptoms have been severe, and have at or almost immediately after the occurrence of the accident attained to their full intensity. Case 1 is an instance of this, and many similar ones must present themselves to the recollection of most surgeons, and there are many such on record.

In these cases, under proper treatment the severity of the symptoms gradually subsides, and, week by week, the patient feels himself stronger and better, until usually in from three to six months at the utmost all traces of the injury have disappeared.

But incomplete or partial recovery is not unfrequent in these cases of severe and direct injury of the spine. Of this, Case 2 is an excellent illustration. The patient slowly recovers up to a certain point and then remains stationary, with some impairment of inner- vation in the shape of partial paralysis of sensation, or of motion, or both, usually in the lower limbs. The intellectual faculties or the organs of sense are more or less disturbed, weakened, or irritated, the constitution is shattered, and the patient presents a prematurely worn and aged look.

In such cases structural lesion of some kind, in the membranes, if not in the cord, has taken place, which necessarily must prevent complete recovery. When, therefore, we find a patient who, after the receipt of a severe injury of the spine by which the cord has been concussed, presents the primary and immediate symptoms of that condition, such as have been described in Case 1, we may entertain a favourable opinion of his future condition, provided we find that there is a progressive amelioration of his symptoms, and no evidence of the development of any inflammation, acute or chronic, of the membranes and the cord.

But our opinion as to his ultimate recovery must necessarily be very unfavourable if we find the progress of amendment cease after some weeks or months, leaving a state of impaired innerva- tion. And this unfavourable opinion will be much strengthened if we find that subsequently to the primary and immediate effect of the injury, symptoms indicative of the development of meningo- myelitis have declared themselves. Under such circumstances of the double combination, of the cessation of improvement and the supervention of symptoms of intra-vertebral inflammatory action, partial restoration to health may eventually be looked for; but complete recovery is not possible.

When a person has received a concussion of the spine from a jar or shake of the body, without any direct blow on the back, or perhaps on any other part of the body, and the symptoms have gradually and progressively developed themselves, the prognosis will always be very unfavourable. And for this reason; – that as the injury is not sufficient of itself to produce a direct and immediate lesion of the cord, any symptoms that develop themselves must be the result of structural changes taking place in it as the consequence of its inflammation; and these secondary structural changesbeing incurable, must, to a greater or less degree, but permanently, injuriously influence its action.

The occurrence of a lengthened interval, a period of several weeks for instance, between the infliction of the injury and the development of the spinal symptoms, is peculiarly unfavourable, as it indicates that a slow and progressive structural change has been taking place in the cord and its membranes, dependent upon pathological changes of a deep-seated and permanently incurable character.

Abercrombie truly says: "Every injury of the spine should be considered as deserv-ing of minute attention, and the most active means should be employed for preventing or removing the diseased actions which may result from it. The more immediate object of anxiety in such cases is inflammatory action; and we have seen that it may advance in a very insidious manner, even after injuries which were of so slight a kind that they attracted at the time little or no attention."

Well, then, when you see a patient suffering from the secondary effects of a slight injury of the spine, these effects having developed in an insidious but progressive manner, examine him with minute attention; and if you find evidence of inflammatory action in the cord and its membranes, as indicated by symptoms of cerebral irritation, spinal tenderness and rigidity, modifications of sensation, as pains, tinglings, and numbness in the limbs, and some loss of muscular or motor power, with a quick pulse and a shattered constitution, you must, at any period of the case, however early, give a most cautious prognosis. And if several months – from six to twelve – have elapsed without any progressive amelioration in the symptoms, you may be sure that the patient will never recover so as – to use the common phrase – " to be the same man" that he was before the accident. But if, instead of remaining stationary, a progressive increase in the symptoms, however slow that may be, is taking place, more and more complete paralysis will ensue, and the patient will probably eventually die of those structural spinal lesions that are described at p. 84.

I have purposely used the words " progressive amelioration" for this reason, that it often happens in these cases that under the influence of change of air, of scene, &c., a temporary amelioration takes place – the patient being better for a time at each new place that he goes to – or under every new plan of treatment that headopts. Fallacious hopes are thus raised which are only doomed to disappointment, the patient after a week or two relapsing, and then falling below his former state of ill-health. . In forming an opinion as to the patient's probable future state, I believe that it is of less importance to look to the immediate or early severity of the symptoms than to their slow, progressive, and insidious development. Those cases are least likely to recover in. which the symptoms affect the latter course.

The time that the symptoms have lasted is necessarily a most important matter for consideration. When they have been of but short duration, they may possibly be dependent on conditions that are completely, and perhaps easily, removable by proper treatment, as for instance, on extravasation of blood, or on acute serous inflammatory effusion (Case 14). But when the symptoms, however slight they may be, have continued even without progressive increase, but have merely remained stationary for a lengthened period of many months, they will undoubtedly be found to be dependent on those secondary structural changes that follow in the wake of inflammatory action, and that are incompatible with a healthy and normal function of the part. I have never known a patient to recover *completely and entirely so as to be in the same state of health that he enjoyed before the accident,* in whom the symptoms dependent on chronic inflammation of the cord and its membranes, and on their consecutive structural lesions, had existed for twelve months. And though, as Ollivier has observed, such a patient may live for fifteen or twenty years in a broken state of health, the probability is that he will die within three or four. There is no structure of the body in which an organic lesion is recovered from with so much difficulty and with so great a tendency to resulting impairment of function as that of the spinal cord and brain. And, with the exception probably of the eye, there is no part of the body in which a slight permanent change of structure produces such serious disturbance of function as in the spinal cord.

Treatment. – I have not much to say to you about the treatment of these injuries that we have been discussing. But I feel that my remarks on this subject would scarcely be complete were I to omit so important a matter from our consideration.

In the early stages of a case of " concussion of the spine," the first thing to be done is undoubtedly to give the injured part complete and absolute *rest.*

The importance of rest cannot be over-estimated in these cases. Without it no other treatment is of the slightest avail, and it would be as rational to attempt to treat an injured brain or a sprained ankle without rest, as to benefit a patient suffering from a severe concussion or wrench of the spine unless he is kept at rest. In fact, owing to the extreme pain in movement that the patient often suffers, he instinctively seeks rest, and is disinclined to exertion of any kind. It is the more important to insist upon absolute and entire rest in these cases, for this reason, that not unfrequently patients feel for a time benefited by movement – by change of air and of scene. And hence such changes are thought to be permanently beneficial. But nothing can be more erroneous than this idea, for the patient will invariably be found to relapse and to fall back into a worse state than had previously existed. In more advanced stages of the disease, when chronic meningitis has set in, the patient suffers so severely from any, even the very slightest movement of the body, from any shock, jar, or even touch, tha$ he instinctively preserves that rest which is needed, and there is no occasion on the part of the surgeon to enforce that which the patient feels to be of imperative necessity for his own comfort.

In order to secure rest efficiently the patient should be made to lie on a prone couch. There are several reasons why the prone should be preferred to the supine position. In the first place, in the prone attitude the spine is the highest part of the body, thus passive venous congestion and determination of blood, which are favoured and naturally occur when the patient lies on his back, are entirely prevented, and that additional danger which may arise from this cause is averted so long as the prone position is maintained. Then again, the absence of pressure upon the back is a great comfort in those cases in which it is unduly sensitive and tender, and is a matter of additional safety to the patient, if he is paraplegic, by lessening the liability to sloughing from undue compression of the soft parts over the sacrum and nates. Lastly, the prone position presents this advantage over the supine, that it admits of the ready application of any local treatment that may be desired to the spine.

In some instances, as in Case 14, complete and absolute rest may be secured to the injured spine by the application of a gutta-percha case to the back, embracing the shoulders, nape, and back of thehead, or, as in Case 13, by letting the patient wear a stiff' collar so as to give the support that is needed to the neck.

But if rest is needed to the spine, it is equally so to the brain. I have repeatedly in these lectures had occasion to point out the fact that in cases of concussion of the spine the membranes of the brain become liable to secondary implication by extension of inflammatory action to them. The irritability of the senses – of sight and hearing, that is so marked in many of these cases – with perhaps heat of head, or flushings of the face, are the best evidences of this morbid action. For the subdual of this state of increased cerebral excitement and irritability, it is absolutely necessary that the mind should be kept as much as possible at rest, and that disquieting influences and emotions should, as far as practicable, be avoided. The patient, feeling himself unequal to the fatigue of business, becomes conscious of the necessity of relinquishing it, though not perhaps without great reluctance, and untfl after many ineffectual efforts to attend to it.

During the early period of concussion of the spine, much advantage will usually be derived from dry cupping along the back on either side of the vertebral column. In some cases I have seen good effects follow the application of ice-bags to the injured part of the spine.

At this period I believe that medicine is of little service beyond such as is required for the regulation of the general health on ordinary medical principles.

When the secondary effects of the concussion of the spine have begun to develop themselves, more scope presents itself for proper medical treatment, and much may often be done not only for the mitigation of suffering, but for the cure of the patient by carefully conducted local and constitutional treatment.

Eest as in the early stages must be persevered in, but in addition to this counter-irritation may now be advantageously employed. With this view the various forms in which this means is familiar to the surgeon – stimulating embrocations, mustard poultices, blisters, and setons or issues – may be successfully employed.

With regard to internal treatment, I know no remedy in the early period of the secondary stage, when subacute meningitis is beginning to develop itself, that exercises so marked or beneficial an influence as the bichloride of mercury in tincture of quinine or of bark. I have seen this remedy produce the most beneficialeffects, and have known patients come back to the hospital to ask for the " bichloride " as the only medicine from which they had derived advantage. At a more advanced period, and in some constitutions in which mercury is not well borne, the iodide or the bromide of . potass in full doses will be-found highly beneficial, more especially when there are indications, as in Case 14, of the presence and the pressure of inflammatory effusion.

When all signs of inflammatory action have subsided – when the symptoms have resolved themselves into those of paralysis whether of sensation or of motion – but more especially in those cases in which there is a loss of motor power, with a generally debilitated and cachectic state, the preparations of nux vomica, of strychnine, and of iron may be advantageously employed. But I would particularly caution you against the use of these remedies, and more especially of strychnine, in all those cases in which inflammatory action is still existing, or during that period of any given case in which there are evidences of this condition. You will find that under such circumstances the administration of strychnine is attended by the most prejudicial effects, increasing materially and rapidly the patient's sufferings. But in the absence of this inflammatory irritation it will, if properly administered, be found to be a most useful remedy, more particularly in restoring lost motor power.

In those cases in which the strychnine may be advantageously administered, great benefit will also be derived from warm saltwater douches to the spine, and galvanism to the limbs.

At a more advanced period of the case, when general cachexy haa been induced, and more or less paralysis of sensation and motion continues in the limbs, and nothing of a specific nature can be done in the way of treatment, our whole object should be to improve the general health on ordinary medical principles, so as to prevent as far as possible the development of secondary diseases, such as phthisis dependent on mal-nutrition and a generally broken state of health, and which may, after a lapse of several years, lead to a fatal termination.

THE END.

Lightning Source UK Ltd.
Milton Keynes UK
15 November 2010

162887UK00002B/330/P